YORK NOTES

THE GREAT GATSBY

F. SCOTT FITZGERALD

Notes by Julian Cowley

PEARSON

YORK
PRESS

YORK PRESS
322 Old Brompton Road, London SW5 9JH

PEARSON EDUCATION LIMITED
Edinburgh Gate, Harlow,
Essex CM20 2JE, United Kingdom

Associated companies, branches and representatives throughout the world

First published 1998
New editions 2004 and 2012
This new and fully revised edition 2015

10 9 8 7 6 5 4 3 2

ISBN 978-1-4479-8228-9

Illustration on page 77 by Alan Batley
Phototypeset by Carnegie Book Production
Printed in Slovakia

CONTENTS

PART ONE: INTRODUCING *THE GREAT GATSBY*

How to use your York Notes to study and revise *The Great Gatsby* 5
The Great Gatsby: A snapshot..6

PART TWO: STUDYING *THE GREAT GATSBY*

Synopsis 8
Chapter 1 10
    Extract analysis: pp. 17–18...14
Chapter 2 16
Chapter 3 18
Chapter 4 22
Chapter 5 26
    Extract analysis: pp. 88–9...28
Chapter 6 30
Chapter 7 34
Chapter 8 38
Chapter 9 40
    Extract analysis: pp. 170–2...42
Progress check 44

PART THREE: CHARACTERS AND THEMES

Characters..46
    Jay Gatsby...46
    Nick Carraway..48
    Daisy Buchanan 50
    Tom Buchanan 52
    Jordan Baker 53
    George and Myrtle Wilson 54
    Meyer Wolfshiem 55
Themes 56
    American ideals 56
    The American Dream 58
    The Frontier...59
    Desire and wonder 60
    Vision and insight 61
    Codes of conduct..62
Progress check 63

PART FOUR: GENRE, STRUCTURE AND LANGUAGE

Genre..64
    Tragedy 64
    Frame narratives..64
Structure 65
    Looking for clues...65
    Intricate patterning..65
Language...66
    The first-person narrator 66
    Dialogue and the scenic method......................................67
    Cinematic techniques..68
    The written word 69
    Symbolism...70
Progress check 71

PART FIVE: CONTEXTS AND INTERPRETATIONS

Contexts 72
    Historical context 72
    Settings 76
    Literary context 78
Critical interpretations 80
    F. Scott Fitzgerald's reputation 80
    Reaction on publication 80
    Subsequent criticism 80
    Contemporary approaches 81
Progress check 83

PART SIX: PROGRESS BOOSTER

Assessment focus 84
How to write high-quality responses 86
Questions with statements, quotations or viewpoints 88
Comparing The Great Gatsby with other texts 90
Using critical interpretations and perspectives 92
Annotated sample answers 94
    Candidate 1 94
    Candidate 2 96
    Candidate 3 98
Practice task 100

PART SEVEN: FURTHER STUDY AND ANSWERS

Further reading 101
Literary terms 102
Revision task answers 103
Progress check answers 104
Mark scheme 112

HOW TO USE YOUR YORK NOTES TO STUDY AND REVISE *THE GREAT GATSBY*

These Notes can be used in a range of ways to help you read, study and revise for your exam or assessment.

Become an informed and independent reader

Throughout the Notes, you will find the following key features to aid your study:

- **'Key context'** margin features: these widen your knowledge of the setting, whether historical, social or political. This is highlighted by the AO3 (Assessment Objective 3) symbol to remind you of its connection to aspects you may want to refer to in your exam responses.
- **'Key interpretation'** boxes (a key part of AO5): do you agree with the perspective or idea that is explained here? Does it help you form your own view on events or characters? Developing your own interpretations is a key element of higher-level achievement in A Level, so make use of this and similar features.
- **'Key connection'** features (linked to AO4): whether or not you refer to such connections in your exam writing, having a wider understanding of how the novel, or aspects of it, links to other texts or ideas can give you new perspectives on the text.
- **'Study focus'** panels: these help to secure your own understanding of key elements of the text. Being able to write in depth on a particular point or explain a specific feature will help your writing sound professional and informed.
- **'Key quotation'** features: these identify the effect of specific language choices – you could use these for revision purposes at a later date.
- **'Progress booster'** features: these offer specific advice about how to tackle a particular aspect of your study, or an idea you might want to consider discussing in your exam responses.
- **'Extract analysis'** sections: these are vital for you to use either during your reading or when you come back to the text afterwards. These sections take a core extract from a chapter and explore it in real depth, explaining its significance and impact, raising questions and offering interpretations.

Stay on track with your study and revision

Your first port of call will always be your teacher, and you should already have a good sense of how well you are doing, but the Notes offer you several ways of measuring your progress.

- **'Revision task'**: throughout the Notes, there are some challenging, but achievable, written tasks for you to do relevant to the section just covered. Suggested answers are supplied in **Part Seven**.
- **'Progress check'**: this feature comes at the end of **Parts Two** to **Five**, and contains a range of short and longer tasks which address key aspects of the Part of the Notes you have just read. Below this is a grid of key skills which you can complete to track your progress, and rate your understanding.
- **'Practice task'** and **'Mark scheme'**: use these features to make a judgement on how well you know the text and how well you can apply the skills you have learnt.

The text used in these Notes is the Penguin Classics edition, 2000.

 PROGRESS BOOSTER

You can choose to use the Notes as you wish, but as you read the novel it can be useful to read over the **Part Two** summaries and analysis in order to embed key events, ideas and developments in the **narrative**.

 PROGRESS BOOSTER

Don't forget to make full use of **Parts Three** to **Five** of the Notes during your reading of the novel. You may have essays to complete on genre, or key themes, or on the impact of specific settings, and can therefore make use of these in-depth sections. Or you may simply want to check out a particular idea or area as you're reading or studying the novel in class.

 PROGRESS BOOSTER

Part Six: Progress booster will introduce you to different styles of question and how to tackle them; help you to improve your expression so that it has a suitably academic and professional tone; assist you with planning and use of evidence to support ideas; and, most importantly, show you three sample exam responses at different levels with helpful AO-related annotations and follow-up comments. Dedicating time to working through this Part will be something you won't regret.

THE GREAT GATSBY: A SNAPSHOT

A novel of its time, or of all time?

The Great Gatsby was published in 1925, yet it continues to capture the imagination of its many readers. The novel's emotional appeal as a love story and its surface glamour have contributed to its popularity, and to the appeal of several film adaptations of the story. Studying this text you will find that it is also a rewarding source of insight into American history and culture, that the subtlety of its narration and characterisation make possible a range of stimulating readings, and that its language has poetic intensity that is rare in a novel. It is a text that can entertain you, but also a work of literary art that invites you to develop your skills of analysis and interpretation. So where might we start to explore its rich potential?

Fitzgerald and a story of the Midwest?

Like the main characters in *The Great Gatsby*, F. Scott Fitzgerald was born in the American Midwest. His family were moderately wealthy, Irish-American and Roman Catholic. He went east to New Jersey to attend Princeton University, a rival in prestige to Yale and Harvard, where he was always conscious that many of his classmates came from well-established families and more wealthy backgrounds. Eventually Fitzgerald moved to Hollywood, on the West coast of America, where he wrote film scripts in order to make money.

The New World and the Old World

The Great Gatsby is a novel about being American and living in the New World. Until a short while before its publication, Fitzgerald wanted the book to be called *Under the Red, White, and Blue*, alluding to the colours of the American flag, commonly known as the Stars and Stripes. But being American has involved a complex relationship with Europe and the values of the Old World, and that is reflected in the novel.

The Jazz Age

Fitzgerald is regarded as the leading chronicler of the Jazz Age. In his novels and short stories, he captured the pleasure-seeking lifestyle of the 1920s in America. This pursuit of pleasure was in part a reaction to the First World War, which seemed to mark the end of an old era. The world was changing, getting faster. There were more and more cars on the roads, telephones allowed instant communication across large distances, and human beings had started to fly in aeroplanes. Electric lighting made homes and public spaces brighter, gramophones turned people's rooms into dance halls, magazines spread gossip about celebrities and moving images of life were projected onto the cinema's silver screen.

Jazz music provided the soundtrack for this new way of life, especially in a modern city such as New York. It was music for young people to dance and party to. Some African-American musicians of the time, such as Louis Armstrong, Bessie Smith, Jelly Roll Morton and Duke Ellington, were great artists and their music has endured. But the dance music in *The Great Gatsby* seems to have been disconnected from its African-American origins. The novel shows America in the Jazz Age divided along lines of race as well as class and gender.

Flappers

The name 'flappers' was applied during the 1920s to young women who lived far more liberated lives than their mothers or grandmothers. Flappers often had their hair cut in a short, boyish bob, and raised the hemlines of their skirts a lot higher than the previous generation would have dared. They wore more make-up and would dance, drink, smoke and drive in a way that some older Americans considered indecent. The emphasis was essentially on greater freedom of movement and behaviour.

A number of Fitzgerald's short stories feature these young and high-spirited flappers. Perhaps the figure closest to a flapper in *The Great Gatsby* is Miss Baedeker, the drunken young woman who tries to slump against Nick's shoulder at Gatsby's party in Chapter 6. Jordan Baker doesn't fit into the flapper category but she is, nonetheless, thoroughly modern – independent, a celebrity sportswoman, and yet sceptical about everything.

Prohibition and organised crime

Between 1920 and 1933 the manufacture, transportation and sale of alcohol in America was prohibited by law. During Prohibition it was not illegal to drink alcohol, but the law was designed to stop people having access to it. Jay Gatsby is said to have made money from bootlegging, the illicit distribution of alcohol. Drunkenness is widespread in this novel.

In Chapter 4 we are shown Gatsby's close association with the criminal gambler Meyer Wolfshiem. During the 1920s, American cities such as New York and Chicago witnessed a great deal of violence as rival gangsters competed for power and influence. Legendary figures such as Al Capone, 'Lucky' Luciano, Meyer Lansky and Dutch Schultz were major players in the criminal underworld.

It was notable that a high percentage of these gangsters were from families who had arrived fairly recently in America – individuals who grew up in energetic Italian, Irish and Jewish communities, and then found that respectable routes to success were denied to them because their backgrounds were so different from that of privileged people like Tom Buchanan.

A02

Study focus: Key issues to explore

As you study the text and revise for the exam, keep in mind these key elements and ideas:

- The character and fate of Jay Gatsby as a reflection of the character and fate of America
- The relationship between the New World (America) and the Old World (Europe)
- The relationship between the present and the past
- The loss of innocence and the capacity to feel wonder
- The reliability of Nick as a **narrator**
- The relationship between **point of view** and truth, or between belief and understanding
- The nature of memory
- The worth of Daisy as the object of Gatsby's love
- The value of hope and dreams in an age of cynicism and materialism
- The value of writing.

In each case, make sure you develop your own interpretations and, with the help of these Notes, prepare to argue your viewpoint on them.

A04 KEY CONNECTION

Fitzgerald's novels portray the 1920s in a far more sombre light than his short stories, which were written for magazine publication and mostly lack the serious concerns of the longer works. The stories have been collected in the volume *Flappers and Philosophers* (Penguin Books, 2010).

A03 KEY CONTEXT

Gender inequality is a notable issue in this novel. Women were not granted the vote in all American states until August 1920. Despite increased independence for women in some areas of life, America remained a patriarchal, male-dominated society.

A03 KEY CONTEXT

A great deal of alcohol is consumed by the pleasure-seekers in this novel, but their drinking often appears irresponsible and even harmful. A sad footnote is that Fitzgerald's own addiction to alcohol undoubtedly contributed to his death at the early age of forty-four.

SYNOPSIS

Nick Carraway narrates

In 1924, Nick Carraway, from the Midwest of the United States, writes an account of certain experiences which affected him deeply while he was working as a bondsman in the New York financial world, a few years earlier. The key events centre upon his next-door neighbour – the glamorous, wealthy and mysterious Jay Gatsby, who is renowned for hosting extravagant parties at his mansion in West Egg village on Long Island.

Love and marriage

Nick visits Daisy Buchanan, a distant relative, and her very rich husband, Tom, whom he had known at university. At their house in East Egg village he meets a young woman named Jordan Baker, who was Daisy's bridesmaid and is now a well-known golfer. Nick and Jordan develop a friendship, which at times has romantic overtones. At one of Gatsby's flamboyant parties, Nick learns from Jordan that Daisy and Gatsby were once in love. They were separated when Gatsby – like Nick himself – was sent to Europe, as a soldier, during the First World War. During his absence overseas, Daisy met and married Tom Buchanan. The Buchanans have a young daughter, Pammy. Jordan also tells Nick that Tom is having an extra-marital affair.

Possession and desire

Five years after their brief love affair, Jay Gatsby remains infatuated with Daisy. He now lives across the bay from her house, and his parties are staged in the hope that they will attract her attention. He wants to win back her love. At Gatsby's instigation, Nick invites Daisy to have tea with him. Gatsby is there too, and he and Daisy are reunited. For a brief period their love seems to flicker back to life. Meanwhile, Tom has introduced Nick to his mistress, Myrtle Wilson, whose husband, George, runs a garage in a bleak district, midway between the city and West Egg.

Tom's affair with Myrtle

Nick visits an apartment in the city that Tom keeps for his affair with Myrtle. The three of them are joined by Myrtle's sister Catherine and a couple called McKee, who live in the flat below. They talk and drink whisky. Myrtle expresses contempt for her husband George, and recalls how impressed she was by Tom's expensive clothes when they first met on a train. Myrtle insists on repeating Daisy's name when she is drunk. In response, Tom breaks her nose.

Gatsby the bootlegger

Nick is intrigued by Gatsby's lifestyle, but disturbed by sinister rumours about his mysterious past. He is said by some to have killed a man; others say he was a German spy during the First World War. The truth emerges that Gatsby has changed his name from James Gatz. He grew up in the Midwest, where his parents unsuccessfully ran a farm. He left home and spent five years travelling with a wealthy prospector named Dan Cody before joining the army and rising to the rank of major. After the First World War, Gatsby moved to the East coast and established contacts in the criminal underworld. Over lunch one day, Gatsby introduces Nick to his friend Meyer Wolfshiem, a criminal who fixed the outcome of the 1919 World Series baseball tournament. It seems that Gatsby, with Wolfshiem's help, became rich through

bootlegging (unlawful distribution of alcoholic drink – the supply of which was prohibited in America during the 1920s). Tom challenges him with this accusation when the two meet at a drinking party at the Plaza Hotel, in New York's Manhattan district.

The death of Myrtle Wilson

After the party at the Plaza, Daisy and Gatsby drive back to Long Island in his car. Earlier that day, George Wilson had told Tom Buchanan that he and his wife Myrtle were planning to move to the West and make a fresh start. Tom was shocked by this news. As Gatsby's car approaches the garage, Myrtle, who has been arguing with her husband, sees the vehicle and mistakenly believes that Tom Buchanan is driving it. She runs into the road, intending to speak with him but she is hit and killed. The car fails to stop. There are witnesses to the incident, including the Wilsons' neighbour, Michaelis. Nick, Tom and Jordan, following in another vehicle, stop at the scene and learn of Myrtle's death. Later, Gatsby tells Nick that he intends to take the blame for the accident, even though Daisy was at the wheel.

The death of Jay Gatsby

Next day, George Wilson, deranged following the death of Myrtle, shoots and kills Gatsby, who is floating on an inflatable mattress in his swimming pool. Wilson then commits suicide. Nick makes all the arrangements for Gatsby's funeral. It is virtually unattended. The Buchanans have left New York. Meyer Wolfshiem says he is unable to be there. Gatsby's father, Henry C. Gatz, arrives from the Midwest, proud (though sadly mistaken) that his son has achieved so much through self-discipline and hard work.

Nick returns to the Midwest

Nick decides to return to the Midwest, where he writes this story, but before leaving the city he meets Tom Buchanan on the street, by chance. Tom admits he told George Wilson that Gatsby was driving the car which killed Myrtle. The novel ends with Nick contemplating his neighbour's house in the darkness, musing on the significance of Gatsby's dedication to his dream, and on the harsh reality which led to his destruction.

A03

Study focus: Modernism

During the early twentieth century, new styles appeared in literature, as in other arts, that became known as modernism. Literary modernism tended to address topics that were controversial and also to experiment with new forms and techniques that often posed a real challenge to readers.

F. Scott Fitzgerald was not an experimental modernist, but he was conscious of language and form, and was aware of advances in **narrative** technique made by early modernist novelists such as Henry James (1843–1916) and Joseph Conrad (1857–1924), both of whom he greatly admired.

A02 PROGRESS BOOSTER

Nick Carraway is a rather low-key participant in the action, but he is also our **narrator**. He has observed events, first hand, and is now writing a book in order to share his observations with us. His role as writer and narrator should be your primary focus when thinking about all aspects of this text.

CHAPTER 1

Summary

- It is 1924. Nick Carraway has returned to the Midwest and is writing a book about events that occurred a couple of years earlier, when he was living on Long Island, New York, in a suburban 'village' (p. 9) called West Egg.
- Nick begins his narration with some self-analysis, trying to pin down aspects of his own character. He also provides a few details about his background. Nick's father runs a family hardware business. Nick himself was sent to France, as a soldier, during the First World War (1914–18).
- Jay Gatsby, Nick's neighbour on West Egg, lives in a mansion. It is a wealthy area. Nick refers to 'the consoling proximity of millionaires', and describes buildings in nearby East Egg as 'white palaces' (p. 11).
- Nick tells of a visit to the house of Tom Buchanan, an acquaintance from Yale University. Tom's wife, Daisy, is Nick's second cousin once removed. Tom Buchanan is physically powerful and extremely rich.
- Nick meets Daisy's friend Jordan Baker, who is a well-known golfer.
- Tom makes racist comments, drawing support for his views from a recently published book, Goddard's *The Rise of the Coloured Empires*.
- Jordan tells Nick that Tom is having an affair with 'some woman in New York' (p. 20). This woman – later we learn that her name is Myrtle Wilson – calls Tom, on the telephone, during dinner.
- Later, in the moonlight, Nick catches his first glimpse of Gatsby, who seems to be captivated by a green electric light shining from the end of the Buchanans' private dock.

Analysis

Past and present

Right at the start of his narration Nick talks about advice he received from his father. Jay Gatsby, we later find out, has turned his back on his parents and has found a very different role model in Dan Cody, his 'mentor'. An important theme in *The Great Gatsby* is the relationship of the past to the present, including what is handed on from one generation to the next. This may take the form of material wealth, but it may also be a set of values, attitudes or expectations.

Study focus: The narrator

Nick Carraway, as the **narrator**, takes the reader into his confidence. He is sharing with us his recollection of certain experiences. At the same time, telling the story, in his own way, is helping him to come to terms with those experiences. Narration helps Nick to explore the significance of events. You will notice immediately that his style can be challenging. Nick's sentences can be grammatically complex, and his vocabulary is at times unfamiliar and even obscure.

Nick is a character in the novel as well as its narrator, and the first person he analyses is himself. His narration is not neutral. Aspects of his character are reflected in the information he offers us, and in the way he presents it. As you read *The Great Gatsby*, watch out for tell-tale clues concerning Nick's own character, and also pay close and critical attention to what he tells us about other characters. Is he a reliable narrator?

We can compare Gatsby's personal history with the history of the American republic, which declared its independence from British rule in 1776. America was asserting itself as a New World, no longer governed by Old World assumptions. America came into existence as a land where anything is possible, and the past is not allowed to set limits.

For a long time, the American West was seen as a place where there was empty space, a kind of blank sheet that Americans could use to start their individual life stories again from scratch. The American West became synonymous with the possibility of a new beginning. Note that both Nick and Gatsby live in West Egg village. The village is geographically located on America's East coast, on Long Island, New York. But the word 'West' links Nick and Gatsby to a widely held belief that life in America is all about hope and possibility. Note that the name 'Egg' seems an additional promise of new life. In the sunshine, on West Egg, Nick has 'that familiar conviction that life was beginning over again with the summer' (p. 10). But the twin Eggs are no more than rocky promontories jutting into Long Island Sound.

War and peace

Nick's great-uncle avoided fighting in the American Civil War (1861–5), and managed to build up a thriving business. Nick and Gatsby, on the other hand, served in the First World War in Europe, after America had joined the conflict in 1917. Gatsby was promoted to the rank of major, an advance in social status that enabled him to make useful connections on the way to getting rich. But one of America's earliest aspirations was to remain a peaceful nation, to avoid war. In that respect it had clearly failed.

Reading Nick Carraway

Note that although the First World War ended in 1918, Nick's move to the East did not occur until 1922. This may reflect the fact that he is not by nature an impulsive person, but it might also suggest that other factors were involved in his decision to move. Perhaps his difficult love affair back home played a larger part than he is willing to admit.

Nick does not present himself as a passionate man, but his imaginative writing style does not seem to match the outlook of a matter-of-fact worker in finance. We may conclude that there are emotional depths to Nick's character that do not feature in the way he openly portrays himself. Ask yourself why Nick is so fascinated by Jay Gatsby that he chooses to tell his story.

A03 KEY CONTEXT

James Gatz breaks away from his past and becomes Jay Gatsby. You might compare this with the way the American colonies broke away from the British Empire. America's Declaration of Independence, issued on 4 July 1776, proclaimed: 'We hold these truths to be self-evident, that all men are created equal, that they are endowed by their Creator with certain unalienable Rights, that among these are Life, Liberty and the pursuit of Happiness.'

New World wealth, Old World status

Nick mentions a belief, held by the Carraway family, that they are descended from the Buccleuchs, upper-class British landowners. In fact, Nick's family runs an unglamorous hardware business selling practical items. In *The Great Gatsby*, we see that despite the Declaration of Independence and the real horrors of the recent war, Europe still attracts wealthy Americans.

Items imported from Europe are an indication of social status. There is much discussion of Gatsby's Oxford education, his Rolls-Royce car, his mansion based on a French town hall and his shirts sent from London. The Buchanans have spent a year in France, not on war service (like Gatsby and Nick), but seeking pleasure. Tom and Daisy's palatial house has a series of French windows and an Italian sunken garden. All these details help to construct an image that seems closer to old-fashioned European aristocratic values than to modern America's democratic ideal.

Note, however, that these wealthy characters live in a distinctively twentieth-century American technological environment. In the 1920s, it was a relatively new world of cars, motorboats, telephones, cinema and electric lighting.

Names and their meaning

Daisy's name evokes a delicate white flower. Nick actually remarks that Daisy opens up 'in a flower-like way' (p. 24). Is this **simile** convincing? Daisy's life seems to be led in an entirely artificial world of wealth and luxury. She seems far removed from the natural world.

Myrtle, who appears in the next chapter, also has a plant's name. In contrast to the delicate daisy, the myrtle is a rather hardy shrub. This plant name seems to suit the tough conditions of Myrtle Wilson's life. But note that, in Mediterranean cultures, myrtle has been associated with love; in the ancient world, myrtle was considered to be sacred to Venus, the goddess of love. Myrtle is, of course, Tom Buchanan's mistress.

Note that Carraway, when spelt 'caraway', is the name of a tall, yellowish plant with thin leaves and seeds that are widely used in cooking. Does this detail tell us anything about Nick? The homely name Carraway certainly seems to place him at a distance from the upper-class dukes of Buccleuch. Buchanan, on the other hand, is actually the name of a Scottish clan who own land near Loch Lomond, in Stirlingshire.

Racial issues

Tom Buchanan's racist comments, bolstered by reference to a recently published book, suggest that America in the 1920s was divided along racial lines, as well as those of social class and gender. American history has often been marked by prejudice and conflict between groups with different cultural or racial backgrounds.

Tom Buchanan considers his own northern European ancestry to be a sure indication of his superiority to people from other backgrounds, especially African Americans, many of whose ancestors were taken by force to work as slaves in the New World. Between the end of the Civil War, in 1865, and the action of this novel, in 1922, many African Americans had moved from the rural South to the major cities and industrial towns of the northern states in search of a new life. The vast majority remained poor and underprivileged.

KEY CONNECTION **A03**

The involvement of Americans in the First World War, alluded to in *The Great Gatsby*, is represented more directly in *A Farewell to Arms* (1929), a novel by Fitzgerald's friend Ernest Hemingway. This love story, set in the context of a military campaign in Italy, is skilfully written to suggest passionate feelings and lives in turmoil by means of language that at times seems emotionally neutral, even numb. Hemingway, like Fitzgerald, used language with great care and refinement.

KEY INTERPRETATION **A02**

In his description of Gatsby's mansion, surrounded by a vast lawn and garden, Nick mentions 'a marble swimming pool' (p. 11). At this point in the **narrative** the pool is a detail that adds to our sense of Gatsby's wealth. But by the end of the novel it takes on more sinister significance, as the location of his death. The glamour turns to tragedy.

Revision task 1: Nick as character and as narrator

A02

Make brief notes setting out what you have learnt so far about Nick. Write about:

● His relationships with other characters in the novel

● His role as narrator

Key quotation: Gatsby's optimism

A01

On page 8, Nick says he is drawn to Gatsby because of his 'extraordinary gift for hope'.

Why should Gatsby's capacity for hope appear so 'extraordinary'? Nick may be reflecting a sense of pessimism, in the aftermath of the First World War, which had shown how easily civilisation and human progress could collapse into savage violence. Gatsby's hopeful nature certainly sets him apart from the cynicism and world-weariness of other characters. It also identifies him with the 'American Dream', in which anything seems to be possible. But the object of Gatsby's hope seems to be to recapture the past. Is that his tragic flaw?

Further key quotations

● During dinner, Tom bursts out 'violently' with the comment 'Civilization's going to pieces.' (p. 18)

● On Daisy and Jordan's chatter: 'as cool as their white dresses and their impersonal eyes' (p. 17)

● Tom on race: 'It's up to us, who are the dominant race, to watch out or these other races will have control of things.' (p. 18)

A03 **KEY CONTEXT**

Nick's great-uncle prospered after avoiding involvement in the Civil War that broke out in 1861 between America's slave-holding southern states, known as the Confederacy, and the more industrial northern states, known as the Union. The Civil War resulted in the abolition of slavery. But more than 600,000 soldiers died and it was one of the first conflicts to use mass-produced weapons. The experience of Americans fighting amongst themselves was deeply damaging to the young nation's self-image.

A04 **KEY CONNECTION**

Tom Buchanan's racism highlights a deep flaw within America's self-image, which numerous writers have addressed, from a variety of points of view. The vicious practice of slave-holding, in the years before the Civil War, is incisively criticised by Mark Twain in *The Adventures of Huckleberry Finn* (1884). An African American's portrayal of the persistence of racist attitudes in American life, and their brutal, oppressive impact upon their victims, can be found in Richard Wright's powerful novel *Native Son* (1940).

EXTRACT ANALYSIS

Chapter 1, pp. 17–18

Reading this passage in isolation, it is easy to forget the important fact that *The Great Gatsby* is first of all a book about a man writing a book. We are not witnessing this scene at first hand, although it may seem on the surface that we are. Nick Carraway is recreating events for us, filtering them through his own personal sense of their significance.

Fitzgerald, the author behind Nick's account, is presenting a scene, set in the Buchanans' house, that involves dramatic **dialogue** between the characters. Such dialogue is an effective means of varying the tone, by introducing the sound of different voices into the narration.

In this way, Fitzgerald prevents Nick's own voice from seeming monotonous or too self-absorbed. Other voices enhance our sense of the characters, and help to develop the storyline. This scene seems complete in itself, but words and actions found here echo and **foreshadow** other words and actions in *The Great Gatsby*. This patterning of the **narrative**, which is often intricate and subtle, creates threads of meaning that result in a rich and complex reading experience, despite the fact that it is not a long novel (see **Part Four: Structure**).

Nick makes reference to Miss Baker. This is the first time he and Jordan have met, so there is a degree of formality. Soon, however, Nick will be calling her by her first name, and before long he will be kissing her. Nick's relationship with Jordan develops in a way that may surprise us, given what he has told us about his reserved character. Can we trust Nick? We learn later that he was still sending letters, at this point, to a girl he had left in the Midwest. We need to watch Nick's character carefully and not simply accept what he tells us.

Jordan and Daisy discuss making a plan, but Jordan is yawning, and Daisy is at a loss, unable to envisage a future that is different from the present. Fitzgerald is portraying the lives of these rich Americans as directionless. They merely drift, feeling that life holds no further possibilities for them. They seem to embody the very opposite of the hopefulness Nick says he values.

Nick notes 'the absence of all desire' (p. 17) in the conversation between Jordan and Daisy. They do not really express or communicate anything, but engage in inconsequential banter. These wealthy women seem to have all they need. Yet their lives lack purpose.

Their eyes are said to appear 'impersonal' (p. 17), no more expressive than their conversation. Eyes, sight and vision form an important thematic thread running through *The Great Gatsby*. At the beginning of the next chapter, those 'impersonal eyes' find an echo in the huge blank stare of Doctor T. J. Eckleburg's advertising hoarding.

Instead of looking to the future, Daisy focuses upon her injured finger. It could be argued that she is essentially a passive figure; things happen to her, and she is content to be shaped by events and other people, rather than controlling her own destiny. She looks at the bruised finger 'with an awed expression' (p. 17). The adjective 'awed' seems entirely inappropriate to this trivial injury. This suggests a lack of proportion in Daisy's judgement, and in her responses. She seems to see life in an exaggerated, distorted fashion. At the same time, the word 'awed' is an example of Fitzgerald's careful verbal patterning; it anticipates the sense of wonder at the heart of Gatsby's enchanted vision.

Daisy's finger has been hurt by her physically powerful husband Tom, although she says it was an accident. The novel contains several other accidents, and numerous allusions to the role of accidental occurrences in human life. This small injury foreshadows a far more disturbing incident in the next chapter, where Tom deliberately breaks the nose of his mistress, Myrtle Wilson, when she drunkenly insists on repeating Daisy's name. Here, Daisy upsets Tom by repeating the word 'hulking'. That parallel in the action strengthens the foreshadowing of Myrtle's injury.

Nick interrupts the dialogue with a brief comment on the distinction between social manners in the American East and the West. Significantly, he says that dinner parties in the East are predictable and drift to an inevitable conclusion, whereas those in the West have plenty of nervous energy, which may result in uncomfortable situations, but at least they have life. Each phase of the Western dinner party is a surge into the uncertain future.

It may seem strange to talk in this way about a meal, but Nick is building a distinction that runs throughout the novel between the hopeful, forward-looking, energetic West and the bored East, trapped in routine and drifting aimlessly.

Note how Nick assumes the role of the unsophisticated rural Midwesterner, asking whether they can talk about crops instead, as that would make him feel more at home. Of course, he has been educated at Yale University, and his casual remarks about the claret – red wine from Bordeaux in France – are a sign of his actual sophistication. Nick often lays claim to a simplicity of character that is clearly at odds with the life he has in fact led.

Tom Buchanan, like Nick, attended Yale. But his racist outburst indicates a kind of ignorance and coarseness. The manner, as well as the content, of his speech conveys a bullying quality, plus a basic lack of intelligence which clashes with his arrogant air of social superiority. In the course of the novel, we discover that Tom has repeatedly committed adultery since he married Daisy. We might ask why Daisy agreed to become this man's wife. Was his wealth the main attraction? Or his physical power? Is Daisy a passive person who merely does what she is told to do?

Daisy and Jordan are dressed in white. Colour symbolism contributes to the narrative patterning of *The Great Gatsby*, and whiteness is one of its principal threads. At times Fitzgerald uses its conventional connotations of purity and innocence, but here 'whiteness' takes on a sinister resonance as the bigoted Tom violently proclaims a need to defend the perceived superiority of the white race.

A02 **PROGRESS BOOSTER**

Pay close attention to Fitzgerald's very careful patterning of words and images. It creates undercurrents of meaning beneath the surface of *The Great Gatsby* that build in strength as the narrative unfolds. Details that initially appear trivial or incidental may acquire unexpected significance. For example, Nick's reference to 'foul dust' floating in the wake of Gatsby's dreams (p. 8) is a **metaphor** that prepares us to recognise the negative connotations of the literal dust that settles on objects, places and people later in the novel.

CHAPTER 2

Summary

- Nick describes a 'valley of ashes' (p. 26), a bleak area between New York City and the suburban village of West Egg. It is watched over by the huge bespectacled eyes of an optician's advertising hoarding.
- Nick is introduced to Tom Buchanan's mistress, Myrtle, the wife of George Wilson, a garage mechanic.
- Tom, Nick and Myrtle catch a train into New York. Myrtle does some shopping and buys a puppy. All three then go to an apartment which Tom and Myrtle use for their extra-marital affair. They are joined by Myrtle's sister Catherine, and by a couple named McKee. They drink whisky and talk until around midnight.
- Tom breaks Myrtle's nose, provoked by her repetition of Daisy's name. Nick leaves with McKee, who insists on showing him some of the photographs he has taken.
- At Pennsylvania Station, Nick waits to catch the 4 a.m. train home.

Analysis

The West and the waste land

The action of *The Great Gatsby* takes place on America's East coast. Nick Carraway is narrating this story after he has moved back home to the Midwest, physically the heart of America. Yet, in the final chapter, Nick says 'this has been a story of the West, after all' (p. 167). He means that it has been a story of the conflict between dreams and the harsh realities of the world, a tale of hope struggling against disillusionment.

For European settlers, arriving on the East coast, America had long been seen as a fresh New World. Moving West, across the continent, was a way to keep that dream alive. Until the last years of the nineteenth century, there were still some areas of land in the American West that hadn't been occupied and settled. But more importantly the West had become a rich symbol of hope, rebirth and unlimited potential to realise your dreams.

On the East coast, in 1922, wealthy New Yorkers drive around in expensive cars, but the unsuccessful garage mechanic George Wilson lives with his wife Myrtle in a dust-covered 'valley of ashes' (p. 26). It is a dismal spot where waste from the city is dumped. They have lived there for eleven years, but now Myrtle has a dream. She longs to leave her past behind and to start a new life with Tom. But in reality Tom has no intention of leaving Daisy; he simply uses Myrtle as his mistress.

Note how Jay Gatsby's dream that Daisy will leave Tom resembles Myrtle's dream that Tom will leave Daisy. Note too that both Gatsby and Myrtle are violently killed – Myrtle by Tom's wife; Gatsby by Myrtle's husband. Are both dreams equally unrealistic? Are Gatsby and Myrtle really in love with Daisy and Tom, or are they simply obsessed with what the Buchanans represent?

The year 1922, in which *The Great Gatsby* is set, saw the publication of T. S. Eliot's *The Waste Land*. That poem registered Eliot's sense that spiritual values had been lost in the increasingly materialistic modern world. Fitzgerald's 'valley of ashes' (p. 26) is literally a waste land, but it can also be read figuratively as an image of a spiritually bleak world.

PROGRESS BOOSTER **A01**

Pay close attention to the locations where the action of *The Great Gatsby* takes place. Fitzgerald does not use geography and landscape simply as background. Think about how these physical settings may contribute to your understanding of the characters and your interpretation of the action.

······
The Gatsby brand
······

We learn that Myrtle was dismayed when she found out that her husband George had borrowed the suit he wore at their wedding (see p. 37). When she first met Tom Buchanan, on a train, she was immediately impressed by his suit, shirt and shoes. Unable to keep her eyes off Tom, she pretended to be looking at an advertisement over his head.

Advertising and brand names were a prominent feature of American life in the 1920s. The huge advertising hoarding, featuring Doctor Eckleburg's bespectacled eyes, is a **realistic** detail from America's early consumer culture. A visual advertisement of this kind couldn't be missed, and it could be understood by newly arrived immigrants with little or no grasp of English language. The optician's hoarding becomes really significant at the end of the novel, when George Wilson – in his bewilderment – mistakes those huge eyes for the eyes of God. Consumerism and materialism have taken the place of spiritual values in the America that Fitzgerald depicts in this novel.

Gatsby's efforts to attract Daisy can be seen as a kind of self-advertisement. He has created an image in order to persuade Daisy that he is the person she needs. In effect he is promoting his own brand. His clothes are imported from Europe, and are intended to impress Daisy just as Tom's clothes impress Myrtle. Note that, in Chapter 8, Daisy actually tells Gatsby that he reminds her of an advertisement (see p. 114).

Progress booster: Celebrity culture (A02)

In recent decades, pop music icons have skilfully used the media to shape their own image and keep themselves in the public view. Long before that, Hollywood film stars also cultivated their image in the press and magazines. Myrtle Wilson reads movie magazines, and follows the celebrity gossip of the day.

When *The Great Gatsby* was published films were still silent, yet Hollywood stars were already world famous. Many Hollywood actors have changed their original name and created a new image. Marilyn Monroe (1926–62), for example, grew up as Norma Jeane Baker.

Try thinking about Jay Gatsby's image in the context of the new celebrity culture of the 1920s, and in terms of what you know about celebrity culture today.

········
Class
········

The Wilsons live over the garage where George works. This shows they have lower social standing than Nick Carraway, who works in the city but lives in a suburb, at a distance from work. The very rich in this novel seem not to work at all, and can live where they choose. Fitzgerald is indicating that America, despite claims to democratic equality, is a society divided into a number of social classes based on wealth and property. He was attracted to the lavish lifestyle of the wealthy, yet he also had a keen sense of social injustice in twentieth-century America.

(A03) KEY CONTEXT

There are strong hints that Gatsby's wealth is due, in part at least, to 'bootlegging', which was the unlawful distribution of alcoholic drinks. The National Prohibition Act, which had been passed in the United States in 1919 and remained in force until 1933, placed severe restrictions upon the manufacture and supply of alcohol.

(A03) KEY CONTEXT

Gatsby's carefully presented image, with all its persuasive trappings of wealth and success, can be understood within the context of recently developed techniques of mass marketing. Susan Strasser's *Satisfaction Guaranteed: The Making of the American Mass Market* (Smithsonian Institute, 2004) is a fascinating and informative account of the development of advertising, a culture of shopping and promotion of brand names in America during the early decades of the twentieth century.

CHAPTER 3

Summary

- Nick describes Gatsby's lifestyle, his servants, lavish parties, motorboats and cars.
- At one of Gatsby's parties, Nick talks with Jordan Baker and two girls she met at an earlier party. They discuss rumours that Gatsby has killed a man, and that he was a German spy in the First World War.
- In Gatsby's library, Nick and Jordan meet a man wearing glasses that make his eyes look owl-like. The owl-eyed man has been 'drunk for about a week' (p. 47).
- Nick meets Gatsby for the first time. Gatsby claims to have seen Nick during their army service in the First World War. They share memories of 'wet, grey little villages in France' (p. 48).
- Gatsby speaks privately with Jordan Baker. She then tells Nick that Gatsby has disclosed 'the most amazing thing' (p. 53).
- Leaving the party, Nick witnesses 'a bizarre and tumultuous scene' surrounding a car that has crashed into a ditch (p. 54).
- Nick's comments on what he has written so far. He remembers a news report which claimed that Jordan Baker had cheated in a golf tournament. He concludes, 'She was incurably dishonest' (p. 58). Nonetheless he admits to feeling 'a sort of tender curiosity' towards her (p. 58).

Analysis

Conspicuous consumption

In Chapter 1, Nick tells us that he drives 'an old Dodge' (p. 9), an ordinary American make of car. Gatsby's British Rolls-Royce and his yellow station-wagon, like his mansion, motorboats, clothes and extravagant parties, mark him out as a rich man. The American sociologist Thorstein Veblen (1857–1929), in his book *The Theory of the Leisure Class: A Study of Economic Institutions* (1899), used the term 'conspicuous consumption' to describe how the rich display their wealth through possessions. Gatsby's lifestyle is a blatant example of 'conspicuous consumption'.

Henry Ford (1863–1947), who pioneered car manufacture in the United States, promoted his cars as democratic vehicles, cheaply produced so that most Americans could afford to run one. Gatsby's expensive cars are part of his plan to impress Daisy; they are meant to stand out from the crowd. Eventually, they play a key role in Gatsby's downfall. Following Myrtle's death in Chapter 7, it is easy for George Wilson to track down the owner of the car that killed her.

The Old World and the New World

We are told that the invitation Gatsby sends to Nick is signed 'in a majestic hand' (p. 43). The notion of majesty, suggested by the adjective 'majestic', belongs to the old-fashioned and traditional social context of European monarchy, not to the dynamic modern world of democratic America. At his parties, Jay Gatsby watches events unfold with the dignity and detachment of an Old World monarch, but at heart he remains a passionate American boy.

KEY CONTEXT (A03)

Jay Gatsby owns a Rolls-Royce car. Engineer Henry Royce (1863–1933) and businessman Charles Rolls (1877–1910) met in Manchester, England, in 1904. Later that year they began to make high-quality cars, designed for the rich and successful. The Rolls-Royce brand was linked from the start with the social elite.

In contrast to Gatsby's cool demeanour, his guests take advantage of every opportunity to have fun 'according to the rules of behaviour associated with an amusement park' (p. 43). Amusement parks were a popular feature of New York life in the 1920s.

Nick is struck by the number of young Englishmen present at the party, 'all well dressed, all looking a little hungry, and all talking in low, earnest voices to solid, prosperous Americans' (p. 43). These young Englishmen resemble characters in the work of Henry James (1843–1916), an American-born novelist who became a British subject in 1915. James wrote many stories and novels in which wealthy yet unsophisticated Americans come into contact with sophisticated yet impoverished Europeans.

The Great Gatsby frequently makes use of this distinction between the energetic and prosperous New World and the Old World, culturally rich yet damaged by war and tired from its long history. The book seems to ask whether America is doomed to repeat Europe's mistakes.

Study focus: Narrative action

A01

The Great Gatsby is a book about a man – Nick Carraway – writing a book about another man – Jay Gatsby – who has remained obsessively in love with a woman – Daisy Fay – whom he met when they were teenagers. Daisy is now married to Tom Buchanan, so a lot of this story is about Gatsby's hope that one day he and Daisy will be together again as lovers. In itself that does not amount to a dramatic, action-packed storyline. Look carefully at the way Fitzgerald creates and connects scenes that hold our attention, rather like a film director who cleverly keeps us watching.

The party in this chapter is part of Gatsby's attempt to impress Daisy. There is plenty of action on the surface: people coming and going, chance meetings, high spirits and drunken behaviour. In itself much of this action is going nowhere, in terms of the development of the story, but as we watch it unfold we are drawn deeper into the heart of Gatsby's obsession.

A03 PROGRESS BOOSTER

It is worth paying attention to the role played by technology in *The Great Gatsby*. In creating a setting for the action of this novel, Fitzgerald made careful use of cars, telephones and electric lighting. We take these things for granted, but they were recent innovations in 1920s America, and they play a significant part in the story.

Revision task 2: Gatsby's parties

A02

Make brief notes outlining the significance of Gatsby's wild parties:

- In terms of your understanding of his character
- In terms of what they tell the reader about New York life in the 1920s

A02 KEY INTERPRETATION

The 'violent confusion' (p. 54) of the comic scene in which a car has crashed into a ditch after leaving the drive of Gatsby's mansion can be seen to **foreshadow** the accident that results in Myrtle Wilson's tragic death. Owl Eyes is here accused of being 'a bad driver' (p. 55), but he reveals that another man was actually driving. Later, Gatsby takes responsibility for Myrtle's death, even though Daisy was driving. Details in this narrative are intricately patterned and intertwined.

Gatsby the showman

Owl Eyes is impressed by the lengths to which Gatsby has gone in creating his image. 'What thoroughness! What realism!' he says, when he discovers that there are actual books on the library shelves rather than just cardboard spines pretending to be books (p. 47). He notes though that the pages remain uncut; these are volumes that have been bought to create an impression rather than to be read.

Nick is part of the story

After describing one of Gatsby's parties at some length, Nick Carraway steps back to examine his telling of the story so far. In doing so, he reminds us of the fact that he is a writer as well as our **narrator**. Events which seem so immediate when we are caught up in the **dialogue** and description have actually been filtered through his remembering and reconstruction of them. Nick is part of the story in a fundamental way. We are learning about Nick as he tells us about Gatsby.

Think about the kind of character Nick says he is. Then look at the way he is writing this story. He presents himself as reserved and rather ordinary. But is that the kind of man you would expect to describe Gatsby's party in sentences such as, 'In his blue gardens men and girls came and went like moths among the whisperings and the champagne and the stars' (p. 41)?

'Most of the time I worked' (p. 56), Nick tells us. His job in New York's financial sector involves selling bonds and reading up on investments. During the day he is surrounded by other office workers, people he knows on first-name terms, who eat run-of-the-mill food in dingy restaurants. Nick enters another world, a world of dreams and imagination, when he meets Jay Gatsby, who hosts lavish parties and provides expensive food and drink for guests he scarcely knows.

Nick tells us he has had a brief affair with a girl, until her brother scared him off. Why should Nick provoke the brother's 'mean looks' (p. 57)? He presents himself as decent, unassuming and respectable and at the end of this chapter he declares, 'I am one of the few honest people that I have ever known' (p. 59). What could the girl's brother find objectionable in such a straightforward and restrained individual as Nick, who keeps his emotions under control and avoids the kind of intense feelings experienced by Jay Gatsby? The two men seem poles apart in temperament. But could it be that Gatsby embodies passion and desire that Nick himself feels, but won't acknowledge?

Study focus: Nick in love

A02

Nick seems to give us a valuable insight into his emotional life when he refers to 'romantic women' (p. 57), whom he chases after, but only in his imagination. Love affairs seem to attract Nick as an idea, but in reality he seems to find it difficult to become fully involved with a woman. He seems to worry that people might find out about his love affairs and disapprove of them. Yet towards the end of the next chapter, Nick puts his arm around Jordan Baker's 'golden shoulder' (p. 77), draws her close to him and invites her to dinner. There seems to be inconsistency here.

As well as his involvement with Jordan, Nick is still in touch with a girl in the Midwest. He tells us: 'I'd been writing letters once a week and signing them: "Love Nick"', and he adds, 'there was a vague understanding that had to be tactfully broken off before I was free' (p. 59). Is Nick being entirely honest with us when he writes of his involvement with women? If not, can we trust his version of events in general?

Key quotation: Interpreting Nick

A02

On p. 59, Nick declares: 'I am one of the few honest people that I have ever known.'

As so often in this novel, an apparently simple statement raises potentially troubling questions. Can we accept that Nick genuinely values truth in a world filled with illusion and deception? Can we trust his assertion that most people he knows are dishonest? Or should we conclude that Nick is deluding himself, or being dishonest with us? Ask yourself how we can be sure of honesty and truth when all the information we receive, as readers, is filtered through Nick's narration.

Further key quotations

- Nick says of his feelings towards Jordan: 'I wasn't actually in love, but I felt a sort of tender curiosity.' (p. 58)
- Jordan says to Nick, 'It takes two to make an accident.' Then she adds, 'I hate careless people. That's why I like you.' (p. 59)
- Nick on his own character: 'I am slow-thinking and full of interior rules that act as brakes on my desires.' (p. 59)

A03 **KEY CONTEXT**

New World borrowings from the Old World are thematically important in this novel. Gatsby's library is Gothic, the dominant decorative style in western European architecture during the Middle Ages. Gothic became fashionable again in Victorian England, and a fusion of Gothic and modern design was popular in America between 1900 and 1930. A notable example is the Woolworth Building, in New York's Manhattan district, known during the 1920s as the Cathedral of Commerce. The decor of Gatsby's library is in keeping with current fashion, but it also reflects his belief that tradition and history are things you can buy.

A03 **KEY CONNECTION**

Note that Jordan's phrase 'careless people' (p. 59) provides the title for Sarah Churchwell's illuminating study *Careless People: Murder, Mayhem and the Invention of* The Great Gatsby (Virago Press, 2013). Starting with a real-life murder mystery, Churchwell delves into events and situations in American life in 1922, the year in which the action of *The Great Gatsby* takes place, and sheds light on circumstances surrounding Fitzgerald's writing of this novel.

CHAPTER 4

Summary

- Gatsby visits Nick for the first time. Nick notices Gatsby's restlessness 'continually breaking through his punctilious manner' (pp. 62–3).
- Gatsby tells Nick about his Midwestern upbringing, his war service, his promotion to the rank of major and his education at Oxford University. Nick senses that Gatsby is not telling the truth. Gatsby alludes to a sad thing that has happened to him.
- Gatsby introduces Nick to Meyer Wolfshiem. Later, Gatsby explains that Wolfshiem illegally fixed the outcome of the 1919 World Series baseball tournament.
- Nick introduces Gatsby to Tom Buchanan. Gatsby makes a sudden departure, clearly embarrassed.
- Jordan tells Nick about the occasion in 1917 when she saw Daisy with Jay Gatsby, then a young lieutenant. Gatsby was then sent to Europe, and was promoted to the rank of major. Meanwhile, Daisy had married Tom Buchanan.
- Jordan tells Nick that she found Daisy, on the day before her wedding, drunk and clutching a letter sent by Gatsby. Soon after the wedding, Daisy became pregnant, and Tom started to have affairs with other women.
- Jordan tells Nick that Gatsby has asked to be invited to his house at a time when Daisy is also present. Nick kisses Jordan.

Analysis

Names and their meaning

The list of guests who visit Gatsby's party is a comic set piece. The tone is quite distinct from the lyrical style that Nick often uses. Note that there are plant names here – 'Hornbeam', 'Endive', 'Orchid', 'Duckweed'; animal names – 'Civet', 'Blackbuck', 'Beaver', 'Ferret', 'Klipspringer'; and names of sea creatures – 'Whitebait', 'Hammerhead', 'Beluga'.

Some of these names make the partygoers seem like caricatures rather than rounded and **realistic** characters. This should draw our attention to the impact a name can have. Remember that *The Great Gatsby* tells the story of a man who has changed his name, for a reason. James Gatz becomes Jay Gatsby so that he may appear to be a more glamorous individual.

KEY CONTEXT   (A03)

Nick wrote his list of visitors to Gatsby's house on a timetable, or schedule, dated 5 July 1922. That calendar detail tells us when the action of this novel took place. It is also the day after Independence Day, when Americans annually celebrate the break with Europe in 1776, which ties in with the book's New World theme.

The Great Gatsby shares its name with its central character. It is important to pay close attention to the names of characters. Remember that the history of America has involved the arrival of immigrants from different parts of the world. You can see from his name that Tom Buchanan has Scottish ancestry, for example, and that Meyer Wolfshiem's family origins are Jewish. Gatz is a Germanic name, and remember that America had recently been at war with Germany. Gatsby is more difficult to pin down in terms of origin. It also has a more sophisticated sound than the monosyllabic Gatz.

Daisy's flowery first name suggests that she is delicate, and physically Daisy appears so. But as we learn more about her character that air of delicacy seems increasingly misleading.

Organised crime

During the 1920s, organised crime had a violent and high-profile impact on life in American cities, such as New York and Chicago. There are numerous suggestions in this novel that Jay Gatsby has strong links with figures from the criminal underworld. His involvement with Meyer Wolfshiem seems to confirm those connections. Wolfshiem is a professional gambler, 'the man who fixed the World's Series back in 1919' (p. 71). Nick thinks of this as a betrayal by one man of the belief in fair play of 50 million baseball fans, an unethical act as well as a major crime performed by Wolfshiem 'with the single-mindedness of a burglar blowing a safe' (p. 71).

Progress booster: Words and meaning

A02

Throughout the novel, Fitzgerald makes his **narrator**, Nick Carraway, use language in unexpected and sometimes peculiar ways. This may be figurative (**metaphor** and **simile**), or poetic, or playful. Watch out for the effects achieved through his use of unusual vocabulary or symbolic language. Think carefully about how Nick's style of storytelling and his choice of words affect your understanding of the story itself and the characters. Is Nick's narrating style part of the novel's more general concern with issues of style and appearance? Can we make a comparison between Nick's words and Gatsby's shirts and suits? Are both designed to project an image, or to conceal something?

A03 **KEY CONTEXT**

Gatsby enhances his social status through war service. In 1840, in *Democracy in America*, the French sociologist Alexis de Tocqueville (1805–59) pointed out that it is possible in a democracy for all soldiers to gain promotion to officer rank, whereas in aristocratic societies rank corresponds strictly to social class. Tocqueville concluded that some Americans would regard war as an opportunity to achieve superior status to their fellow citizens.

A05 **KEY INTERPRETATION**

A New Historicist reading of the novel might focus on Wolfshiem's Jewish identity and point out that prominent American gangsters during the 1920s often came from non-Anglo-Saxon backgrounds. 'Bugsy' Siegel and Meyer Lansky came from Eastern European Jewish families; Al Capone was a son of Italian immigrants; Dean O'Bannion and his North Side Mob in Chicago were Irish Americans. A reason for their criminality might be that they found lawful routes to success blocked to them because of their ethnic origins.

KEY CONTEXT **A03**

The Great Gatsby is a novel that shows the actual conditions of people's lives in America to be at odds with the nation's ideals and aspirations. Further insight into the disparity between the ideal and the actual may be gained from Howard Zinn's *A People's History of the United States* (Harper Perennial Modern Classics, 2010).

PROGRESS BOOSTER **A01**

When you comment on events or characters in this novel, bear in mind that Nick is presenting them to us. Pay attention not only to what he writes about, but also to the way he writes. For example, Nick describes Wolfshiem eating 'with ferocious delicacy' (p. 69); and he remarks that Gatsby bought a mansion, 'from which he dispensed starlight to casual moths' (p. 76). Take note of his style and vocabulary. What kind of a storyteller is Nick Carraway? Always remember, however, that F. Scott Fitzgerald is behind the scenes, creating Nick, along with the other characters.

Starting afresh

As Gatsby drives him from Long Island to Manhattan, crossing the East River, Nick observes: 'The city seen from the Queensboro Bridge is always the city seen for the first time, in its first wild promise of all the mystery and the beauty in the world' (p. 67). This reaction to New York **foreshadows** the passage in the final chapter where Nick imagines a Dutch sailor seeing for the first time the 'fresh green breast of the new world' (p. 171). America seemed to offer Europeans a chance to start afresh. Nick still feels the sense of a new beginning as he enters New York City. When Nick grasps the intense nature of Gatsby's love for Daisy, and realises that his neighbour has bought a mansion in order to live across the bay from her, he remarks, 'He came alive to me, delivered suddenly from the womb of his purposeless splendour' (p. 76). Nick has regarded him as a flashy character, but Gatsby is now reborn for him as a passionate man with deep feelings and a purpose in life.

Youth

Note that in 1917, when Gatsby first met her, Daisy was just eighteen. Jordan was only sixteen at that time. So in 1922, when the action of the novel takes place, they are both still young. Jordan is just twenty-one, yet she is cynical and is said to be dishonest and a cheat. Despite these character flaws, Nick is clearly attracted to her.

Nick likes to present himself as a detached and rather cold person, who at thirty is too old for youthful excitement and strong feelings. Yet here he physically holds and kisses Jordan Baker. Gatsby, clinging to his memories of an adolescent love affair with Daisy, remains alone, living in hope. On the other hand, Nick's involvement with Jordan may seem opportunistic and unromantic.

America has cultivated an image as a youthful nation, full of energy and hope. Remember though that the New World settled by European immigrants had for centuries before their arrival been inhabited by Native Americans. The Europeans took the land, often by force. That fact, and the enslavement of Africans until the mid nineteenth century, reveals a violent reality underlying America's youthful self-image.

Revision task 3: Dishonesty and injustice   **A02**

Identify five or more details or events in the novel which suggest that America is a land of dishonesty and injustice.

Key quotation: Nick's perception of Gatsby   **A01**

On page 76 Nick writes that, after Jordan reveals that Gatsby bought his house to live across the bay from Daisy, 'He came alive to me, delivered suddenly from the womb of his purposeless splendour.'

This image of delivery from a womb connects with other images of birth and new beginnings that have important thematic significance within *The Great Gatsby*. Note that until this point Nick has regarded Gatsby's display of wealth as 'purposeless'. The revelation that Gatsby is motivated by love for Daisy differentiates his life from the apparently purposeless lives led by other wealthy characters in the novel. This is the moment when Nick starts to see Gatsby as a romantic hero. Does he perhaps recognise in Gatsby romantic tendencies that linger unfulfilled within his own character?

A03 **KEY CONTEXT**

The character Meyer Wolfshiem is modelled on a real-life gangster named Arnold Rothstein (1882–1928). In 1919, the Chicago White Sox baseball team took bribes, financed largely by Rothstein, and allowed the Cincinnati Reds to win the World Series tournament. This was one of America's biggest sporting scandals.

Further key quotations

- Gatsby identifies Meyer Wolfshiem as 'the man who fixed the World's Series back in 1919'. (p. 71)
- Nick of Gatsby: 'I wondered if there wasn't something a little sinister about him, after all.' (p. 64)
- Gatsby says, 'I lived like a young rajah in all the capitals of Europe.' (p. 64)
- Wolfshiem says that Gatsby is 'very careful about women. He would never so much as look at a friend's wife.' (p. 70)

CHAPTER 5

Summary

- When Nick gets home, at two o'clock the next morning, he finds that Gatsby's house is brightly lit.
- Gatsby – still awake – talks with him, discussing his plan to meet Daisy at Nick's house.
- On the day arranged for Gatsby's meeting with Daisy, it rains heavily. While Gatsby and Daisy talk, Nick wanders into his garden and looks at the neighbouring mansion, Gatsby's home.
- When Nick returns to the room he notices that Daisy has been crying.
- Nick and Daisy go with Gatsby to look at his house. It is filled with items imported from Europe, including clothes sent from England. Daisy is overwhelmed by Gatsby's 'beautiful shirts' (p. 89).
- Nick is struck by the intensity of the relationship between Gatsby and Daisy. After a while, he leaves them alone together.

Analysis

Let there be light

Nick describes Gatsby, glowing after his conversation with Daisy, as 'an ecstatic patron of recurrent light' (p. 86). This is poetic language, rich with potential meaning. It makes Gatsby seem an extraordinary figure, with an almost god-like capacity to dispense light or restore sunshine after the rain. Earlier, on a more mundane level, we have witnessed Gatsby's extravagant use of electric lighting in his house and at his parties.

Nick compares Gatsby's mansion, ablaze with light, with the World's Fair (see p. 79). Fitzgerald was probably referring specifically to the International Exposition of Science, Arts and Industries held in the Bronx area of New York City in 1918. This combined an amusement park with exhibitions showing the latest scientific and technological innovations. Such events are designed not only to educate and entertain the public, but also to promote the image of the host nation.

We might choose to read the blazing lights of Gatsby's house as an image of his blazing love for Daisy. Or we may see it as a form of display, using electricity as he uses his cars and clothes in the hope of attracting Daisy's attention and drawing her to him. Note that, later in this chapter, in sunshine following a spell of rain, Gatsby remarks to Nick: 'My house looks well, doesn't it?' and he adds 'See how the whole front of it catches the light?' (p. 87).

KEY CONTEXT **A03**

Electric lighting provides illumination for several scenes in *The Great Gatsby*. It was in 1878 that Thomas Alva Edison (1847–1931), inventor of the incandescent light bulb, announced to a world then lit by gas that it was possible to install domestic electric lighting. In the same year that Edison invented the phonograph and opened up the world of sound recording, he also made major contributions to development of the telephone and motion-picture camera. Such inventions transformed American life in the early twentieth century, and that is registered in this novel.

Europe and America

Gatsby's mansion has a 'feudal silhouette' (p. 88), like a building from the feudal society of the European Middle Ages. But **ironically** that silhouette is cast by modern electric lighting. The mansion was built by a brewer who wanted to live like an Old World lord of the manor, with his loyal workers housed in old-fashioned straw-thatched cottages. But note that the American workers refused to accept the straw roofs; they are not Old World peasants.

In medieval feudal life, the relationship between the ruling class and the peasantry was unchanging. People accepted their place in society. In a modern democracy with a capitalist economy, the opposite is the case. Individuals are socially mobile. The brewer presumably lost his fortune when Prohibition prevented the manufacture of alcohol. Ironically, Jay Gatsby, who is allegedly a bootlegger, distributing alcohol illegally, has taken the brewer's place in the feudal mansion.

Gatsby tells Nick that he made enough money to buy this mansion in just three years. That expenditure would have been far beyond the income of most workers in 1920s America. Nick observes, 'Americans, while willing, even eager, to be serfs, have always been obstinate about being peasantry' (p. 86). Nick seems to be suggesting that while Americans are prepared to do routine work – as George Wilson does – they will not accept the role of peasants, with no hope of changing and improving the condition of their own lives.

A self-made man, like Gatsby, would have been unthinkable in a feudal society, where everyone accepted their place in the social hierarchy. Nonetheless he seems to have made his money illegally, and importations from the Old World play a large part in his display of wealth. It's a complicated picture, with the Old World still clearly exerting an influence on New World thinking.

A02

Progress booster: *The Great Gatsby?*

The title *The Great Gatsby* creates certain expectations, making us eager to find out what makes Gatsby special. He stands out because of his wealth. But there are strong hints that he is rich because he is a criminal. Also, he is driven by his desire to steal away another man's wife. Ask yourself in what ways Jay Gatsby deserves to be called 'Great'. Pay careful attention to the way Fitzgerald handles the reunion between Daisy and Gatsby, a difficult scene to manage. Throughout the novel you should look out for ways in which the author is guiding the way we respond to Jay Gatsby.

A02

Revision task 4: Gatsby in love

Make notes identifying ways in which your understanding of the characters of Gatsby and Daisy develops during the course of this chapter.

A05 KEY INTERPRETATION

A New Historicist reading of *The Great Gatsby* might approach it as a document of its time, shedding light on ways in which human behaviour and social relationships were modified by the technological changes that occurred during the opening decades of the twentieth century. The presence of cars and telephones in the novel might be read as evidence of changing spatial awareness, with physical distance being diminished by increased speed and remote communication.

A01 PROGRESS BOOSTER

Many novels aim to present **realistic** action and characters. Think carefully about how writers create a sense of realism, piling up descriptive details, dates, names and other references that make you feel you are in a solid and familiar world. *The Great Gatsby* presents a familiar world up to a point, but Fitzgerald gives us the workings of Nick Carraway's memory and imagination rather than straightforward, uncomplicated facts.

EXTRACT ANALYSIS

Chapter 5, pp. 88–9

The episode in which Gatsby and Daisy, reunited for a few hours after five years apart, visit his mansion carries an enormous amount of weight in the novel. Fitzgerald has already indicated to us that the real Daisy falls far short of the idealised Daisy who exists in Gatsby's heart and imagination. Now the author has to ensure that the encounter between these two characters is convincing.

Gatsby and Daisy have a lot of catching up to do. We might expect to hear them talk at length. Fitzgerald was a skilful writer of **dialogue**, but he keeps their conversation to a minimum. Their feelings are communicated through the way they act in this emotionally charged situation. We need to read their body language, to interpret their physical movements, which are notably awkward at first, and to be aware of what remains unsaid.

Daisy has never attended any of Gatsby's parties, so his mansion has the attraction of a new experience, the magic of a first encounter. Nick, on the other hand, feels the strangeness of being at the house without other guests. The relationship between the present and the past is thematically important to the novel as a whole, and it is particularly significant in this chapter, where we might expect the reunion of Gatsby and Daisy to be saturated with memories of their brief but intense love affair, five years earlier.

The description of Gatsby's mansion is highly economical yet it conveys his immense wealth and his painstaking stage management, with everything arranged in order to impress Daisy. Just before this passage, Daisy, with her floral name, has admired Gatsby's garden. Note that he has even taken pains over the scent of flowers growing there, 'the sparkling odour of jonquils and the frothy odour of hawthorn and plum blossoms and the pale gold odour of kiss-me-at-the-gate' (p. 88). The adjectives 'sparkling', 'frothy' and 'pale gold' suggest the fizz and colour of a glass of champagne.

In this passage Gatsby shows Daisy and Nick the upstairs rooms in his mansion. Here there are 'period bedrooms swathed in rose and lavender silk' (p. 88), imitating the luxury of an earlier historical period. Already, downstairs, we have encountered music-rooms in the style of Marie Antoinette. It also has Restoration salons; rooms in the style of the age of Charles II.

In Gatsby's own apartment we discover he has not only a bedroom and a bath, but also a study. Owl Eyes told us in Chapter 3 that the pages of books in Gatsby's library remain uncut; despite a brief spell at Oxford University in reward for his war service, Gatsby is clearly not a studious man. But a study fits the sophisticated, aristocratic image this young man from the Midwest has tried to cultivate. The room is said to be in the elegant eighteenth-century architectural style of the Scottish brothers Robert Adam (1728–92) and James Adam (1730–94).

KEY CONTEXT **A03**

The historical allusions in *The Great Gatsby* are carefully chosen to enrich its meaning. Marie Antoinette was a French queen who was executed by revolutionaries in 1793. Charles II (1630–85) was restored to the English throne in 1660. His father, Charles I (1600–49), had been executed during the English Civil War by revolutionary forces under the leadership of Oliver Cromwell (1599–1658). It is **ironic** that signs of status in democratic America in the 1920s involve 'period bedrooms' and other imitations of the style of European monarchies overthrown by violent revolution.

The Adam brothers were historical figures, but words in *The Great Gatsby* often trigger associations in ways that enrich meaning. The surname Adam might trigger an association with Adam in the Bible. Jay Gatsby, beginning his life afresh, might in some respects remind us of Adam, the first man created by God in a brand new world. Daisy might then be viewed in **archetypal** terms as Eve, tempting Adam to lose his innocence, with tragic consequences. The artificial, stage-managed world that Gatsby inhabits is, however, no Garden of Eden.

Gatsby, Nick and Daisy drink Chartreuse, a bright green liqueur. Note how this small detail, like many others, resonates with major themes of the novel. Its greenness fits into the novel's careful patterning of colours. It may remind us of the green light that burns all night at the end of Tom and Daisy's boat dock, and it anticipates the powerful image in the final chapter of a Dutch sailor encountering for the first time 'a fresh, green breast of the new world' (p. 171). Green suggests natural life and growth, and also a kind of innocence. In Gatsby's carefully cultivated world, however, grass is trimmed, flowers are cut and herbs flavour an alcoholic drink. Significantly, in America 'green' is slang for money, as it has historically been the colour of the dollar banknote.

Gatsby is overwhelmed with emotion during Daisy's visit. When she uses his gold brush to smooth her hair, he watches, spellbound, trying to speak but unable to find the words to express his feelings. Nick observes that Gatsby 'was consumed with wonder at her presence' (p. 89). Note that the Dutch sailor, encountering 'a fresh, green breast of the new world' in the final chapter is said to have been a human being 'face to face for the last time in history with something commensurate to his capacity for wonder' (p. 171).

Is Fitzgerald suggesting that the awesome vision of America as a New World, with apparently limitless potential, has narrowed down to a point where wonder is no more than what Gatsby feels as he watches Daisy brush her hair in his bedroom? Or is that capacity for wonder perhaps the source of Gatsby's 'greatness'? Is it his sense of wonder that drives him to refuse to live the aimless and unsuccessful kind of life led by his parents?

When the intensity of Gatsby's feelings leaves him unable to speak coherently, his props come to the rescue. He opens two large cabinets that contain his clothes, declaring that he employs a man in England to buy them for him. Expensive linen, silk and flannel shirts are thrown in front of Daisy and Nick as symbols of Gatsby's success and sophistication. They take the place of words as a means to communicate with the woman he loves. As we know, in our own fashion-conscious times, the clothes you wear make a statement about the person you are, or think you are. But is it always the statement we intend to make? Others might read it differently. We might interpret the 'many coloured disarray' (p. 89) of Gatsby's shirts as nothing more than a disclosure of the turmoil of his inner life.

In response Daisy cries 'stormily' (p. 89). Note the turbulence implied by that adjective. Why should a collection of fashion items create a storm within Daisy? She offers an explanation: 'It makes me sad because I've never seen such – such beautiful shirts before' (p. 89). As readers we are left to conclude that, while our attention is directed to these beautiful shirts, the hearts of two former lovers are beating in deep disarray.

A03 KEY CONTEXT

R. W. B. Lewis's classic study *The American Adam: Innocence, Tragedy, and Tradition in the Nineteenth Century* (University of Chicago Press, 1955) identifies Jay Gatsby as one among many American literary characters who have invited comparison with the biblical figure of Adam.

A04 KEY CONNECTION

With the allusions in this novel to European history and culture, compare the experiences of Isabel Archer, an American living in the Old World, in *The Portrait of a Lady* (1881) by Henry James. The manner in which relationships between Europeans and Americans were affected by differences of national character, value and perception was a major theme in James's fiction.

A05 KEY INTERPRETATION

A post-colonial critical reading of *The Great Gatsby* might focus upon ways in which wealthy Americans, despite their nation's revolutionary break from European imperialism, continue to emulate Old World models when wishing to display their wealth or social success. Such an analysis might suggest that Americans have internalised values from the European past, and in that respect remain subject to Old World power.

CHAPTER 6

Summary

- Nick tells us that an inquisitive newspaper reporter visited Gatsby one morning; rumours about him had spread to a point where 'he fell just short of being news' (p. 94).
- Nick then tells us what he knows of Gatsby's real life-story. His original name was James Gatz and he grew up in North Dakota.
- At seventeen James Gatz changed his name to the more glamorous Jay Gatsby.
- He met Dan Cody, who had become wealthy prospecting for precious metals. Cody became Gatsby's mentor, teaching him how to get rich.
- Nick tells us about an occasion when Tom Buchanan visits Gatsby's mansion. Gatsby tells Tom that he knows Daisy.
- Tom and Daisy Buchanan attend a party at Gatsby's mansion.
- Gatsby and Daisy spend half an hour together, sitting on the steps of Nick's house.
- Tom suggests to Nick that Gatsby is a criminal bootlegger, like a lot of newly rich Americans at that time.
- Gatsby is upset that Daisy has not enjoyed the party. He wants her to leave her husband and marry him.

Analysis

Being and becoming

In his first novel, *This Side of Paradise* (1920), Fitzgerald writes of his main character, a young man named Amory Blaine: 'It was always the becoming he dreamed of, never the being.' In *The Great Gatsby*, we are told that Jay Gatsby's parents lived in one place, and worked within the fixed pattern of a farming life. His parents were solidly 'being' themselves. Gatsby, on the other hand, dreams, like Amory Blaine, of 'becoming' someone. He does not want his identity to be pinned down.

Nick tells us that Gatsby was the son of 'shiftless and unsuccessful farm people' (p. 95). His parents lived off the land, but to him their lives seemed aimless. At seventeen, Gatsby met Dan Cody, who lived on a yacht and was a millionaire. As farmers, his parents had a fixed place to live and work; Cody, on the other hand, was mobile and energetic and that attracted Gatsby. He left his parents behind – 'his imagination had never really accepted them as his parents at all' (p. 95) – and went off with Cody, who showed him another way of living a life.

KEY CONNECTION **A04**

During the last quarter of the nineteenth century, discovery of easily collected mineral ores drew many to prospecting; Fitzgerald's fictional Dan Cody was one of the lucky few. Note that in the first chapter of Book II of Willa Cather's *My Ántonia* (1918) we are told that the character Jake Marpole became a prospector, dreaming that a silver mine awaited him in Colorado.

Nick tells us that, when he met him, there was a persistent rumour that Gatsby 'didn't live in a house at all, but in a boat that looked like a house and was moved secretly up and down the Long Island shore' (p. 94). This rumour, though untrue, should remind us of Gatsby's earlier life on Cody's yacht, which had represented for him 'all the beauty and glamour in the world' (p. 96). It should also remind us of Gatsby's determination not to be fixed in place and identity like his parents.

When Europeans started to arrive in America and decided to establish farming communities, they were often referred to as 'settlers'. America's past is a history of settlement. But it is also a history of restless movement.

Idealism and materialism

Nick tells us, 'The truth was that Jay Gatsby of West Egg, Long Island, sprang from his Platonic conception of himself' (p. 95). Plato was an ancient Greek philosopher who argued that there is an ideal world beyond the material world in which we live. Our human senses are too crude to grasp this ideal world. The suggestion here is that seventeen-year-old Jay Gatsby, unhappy with his material circumstances, has created an ideal version of himself. His dreams and vivid imaginings have convinced him of 'the unreality of reality' (p. 95). His ideal has become more real to him than the physical world around him.

Gatsby was introduced to a wealthy lifestyle by the highly materialistic Dan Cody, and has developed his own image on the basis of material success achieved through illegal activity. Cody became a millionaire, but Nick tells us that under the surface he remained 'the pioneer debauchee, who during one phase of American life brought back to the Eastern seaboard the savage violence of the frontier brothel and saloon' (p. 97). A pioneer might seem heroic, but Fitzgerald reminds us that actual life at the Frontier was often violent and dangerous.

A01

Progress booster: The role of accidents

In this chapter, James Gatz seems to seize control of his own destiny when he changes his name and starts to create a new life as Jay Gatsby. But it was his chance meeting with Dan Cody that really made the difference, and in Chapter 8, Gatsby acknowledges that it was a 'colossal accident' (p. 141) that led him to Daisy Fay's house.

In Chapter 1, Daisy asks Nick, 'What do people plan?' (p. 17). Jay Gatsby tries to plan the course of his life; he tries to design events in order to win Daisy's love. But his plans end in disaster. Several accidents occur in this novel – notably car crashes. Pay close attention to plans made by characters in *The Great Gatsby*, and to the role of accidents in the **narrative**.

A02

Revision task 5: Role models

Make notes setting out what you have learnt in this chapter concerning:

● Gatsby's dissatisfaction with the lifestyle of his parents
● The attraction for Gatsby of Dan Cody as a role model

A03 **KEY CONTEXT**

Gatsby is said to spring from 'his Platonic conception of himself'. In *The Republic*, his blueprint for a model society, the Greek philosopher Plato (*c.*427–347 BC) argues that the material world is illusory; our physical senses are too crude to grasp the true nature of reality, which exists in ideal forms. In Plato's republic, divisions of social class are rigid. It is impossible for members of the warrior or working classes to adopt the lifestyle of the aristocracy, whose souls are superior.

Study focus: A kind of magic

A02

As Daisy sings, Nick hears in her husky voice 'a little of her warm human magic' (p. 104). Nick then imagines the arrival of some radiant young woman who might make Gatsby forget his years of devotion to Daisy, in 'one moment of magical encounter' (p. 105). The term 'magic' is here used to refer to that strange quality of attraction often described as a form of enchantment, or associated with falling under a spell.

A more down-to-earth kind of magic might be suggested by the name 'The Great Gatsby'. It is the kind of name often adopted by stage magicians and illusionists. Is Gatsby, after all, no more than a showman, dealing in illusions? Or can we detect another kind of magic in the way that he transforms himself from an ordinary Midwestern boy into a glamorous man of mystery? Or when he transforms Daisy Fay, within his own imagination, from a pretty Louisville girl to an ideal of radiant life and beauty?

Time passes

Nick warns, 'You can't repeat the past'. Gatsby replies, 'Why of course you can!' (p. 106). This is an illustration of Gatsby's 'extraordinary gift for hope' (p. 8), but we can see that he is deluded. The future he imagines for himself is actually focused in a moment that is forever lost in the past, the magical moment when he fell in love with Daisy Fay.

Remember that Gatsby has tried to delete much of his past; to erase all traces of his family and his upbringing in the Midwest. But the last words of the final chapter of *The Great Gatsby* confirm that we can never escape the flow of time: 'So we beat on, boats against the current, borne back ceaselessly into the past' (p. 172). That sentence is carved into Fitzgerald's gravestone.

KEY CONTEXT **A03**

James Gatz is said to 'invent' Jay Gatsby. Fitzgerald's English contemporary D. H. Lawrence (1885–1930), in his *Studies in Classic American Literature* (1923), identifies 'plumbing' and 'saving the World' as 'the two great American specialities'. Lawrence makes a connection between the practical and the visionary aspects of American culture by suggesting that American skill at invention, especially of labour-saving machines, has resulted in more free time for dreaming.

Progress booster: Memories and dreams

A01

In Chapter 5, Gatsby, who is emotionally drained by his reunion with Daisy, is said to be 'running down like an over-wound clock' (p. 89). In Chapter 6, an old clock ticks on young Jay Gatsby's washstand (p. 95). Clocks measure the passing of the hours mechanically, but you should be aware of the important and unmeasurable role played within Gatsby's sense of time by memories and dreams.

A sense of wonder

His love for Daisy makes Gatsby feel that he can 'suck on the pap of life, gulp down the incomparable milk of wonder' (p. 107). The image is of a child at its mother's breast, being nourished with the 'milk of wonder'. 'Wonder' is a key word in this novel.

This image of 'the pap of life' **foreshadows** the reference at the end of *The Great Gatsby* to 'a fresh, green breast of the new world', a vision that can match the human 'capacity for wonder' (p. 171).

Note that between these moments of wonder, however, Myrtle Wilson is hit by a car, and we are told that 'her left breast was swinging loose like a flap' (p. 131). This is a shocking image of a literal rather than a figurative breast. *The Great Gatsby* is a novel in which the material world is repeatedly shown to be in conflict with visionary ideals.

Key quotation: Gatsby's parents **A02**

On page 95, Nick describes Gatsby's mother and father: 'His parents were shiftless and unsuccessful farm people – his imagination had never really accepted them as his parents at all.'

The word 'shiftless' here means lacking in ambition, but it also suggests that Henry Gatz and his wife were unable to 'shift', stuck in one place, physically and in terms of social advancement. Note that on page 34 Nick writes, with biting **irony** in terms of class distinctions, 'Myrtle raised her eyebrows in despair at the shiftlessness of the lower orders.' In that instance 'shiftlessness' means 'laziness'. Pay close attention to Nick's careful use of vocabulary to produce shades and nuances of meaning.

Further key quotations

- Nick on Gatsby: 'So he invented just the sort of Jay Gatsby that a seventeen-year-old boy would be likely to invent, and to this conception he was faithful to the end.' (p. 95)
- Gatsby's daydreams were a 'promise that the rock of the world was founded securely on a fairy's wing'. (p. 96)
- Tom: 'I may be old-fashioned in my ideas, but women run around too much these days to suit me.' (p. 100)
- Gatsby knew that when he kissed Daisy 'and forever wed his unutterable visions to her perishable breath, his mind would never romp again like the mind of God.' (p. 107)

A01 **PROGRESS BOOSTER**

Think carefully about the relationship between fact and fiction in this novel. What are the facts? What do we actually know for sure? Gatsby has changed his identity and is surrounded by gossip and rumour. Nick is our guide to the events and characters in this story, but how far can we trust him? Can we assume that what Gatsby has told him about his earlier life is true? It is important to show that you recognise that the truth is not straightforward in *The Great Gatsby*.

A03 **KEY CONNECTION**

With the restlessness of young James Gatz, and his need to leave behind his parents' farm, compare Huck Finn's inability to accept a settled domestic lifestyle at the end of Mark Twain's *The Adventures of Huckleberry Finn* (1884). You find comparable characters in the American 'road movie', a cinematic genre that is as much about a restless state of mind as it is about motor cars. The basic fear in such stories seems to be that once you settle you cease to dream. What signs are there that Gatsby has not really settled in his house on West Egg?

CHAPTER 7

Summary

- Daisy has been visiting Gatsby regularly. He has dismissed his servants to prevent the spread of gossip.
- On the hottest day of the summer, Nick and Gatsby have lunch with the Buchanans. They meet Daisy's daughter, Pammy. Tom recognises that Daisy and Gatsby are in love.
- They drive into New York: Tom takes Nick and Jordan; Gatsby travels with Daisy.
- Tom stops for petrol at George Wilson's garage, and is startled to learn that the Wilsons plan to go West.
- Tom, Daisy, Jordan, Nick and Gatsby take a room in the Plaza Hotel. Gatsby asserts that he is the only man Daisy has ever really loved. Tom scornfully alludes to Gatsby's links with the criminal underworld.
- The **narrative** cuts to an inquest where Michaelis, the Wilsons' neighbour, is a witness.
- Myrtle Wilson has been killed by a hit-and-run driver. A bystander testifies that the 'death car' was a big yellow vehicle (p. 131).
- In the garden of the Buchanans' home, Gatsby tells Nick that Daisy was driving the vehicle, and discloses that he intends to take the blame for Myrtle's death.

Analysis

KEY INTERPRETATION A03

There is an unlikely parallel between Myrtle glimpsing a previously unknown world in Tom's lifestyle and Gatsby discovering a new world in Daisy Fay's family background. Both Myrtle and Gatsby are from a lower social class, and both are dazzled by wealth and glamour that they want to make their own. Gatsby sends a photo of his house to Henry C. Gatz; Myrtle places her mother's photo on the wall of the apartment where she commits adultery with Tom. What should we make of the connection these photographs form with the past of each character?

Study focus: The heat of the day A02

A less skilful writer may have merely mentioned that the action in this chapter took place on the hottest day of the year. Fitzgerald uses the intense heat of the day to enrich the meaning of the story. The heat drains energy from the characters, yet the restless Buchanans still drive into the city. The wedding party at the Plaza hotel prompts the Buchanans to reminisce about another very hot day on which they were married. The heat makes people irritable and uncomfortable, and brings problems and disagreements to the surface. It intensifies the tensions that are developing in the novel. Just as location is important in this novel, so too is the weather in this chapter. Pay close attention to the ways in which Fitzgerald makes the heat seem completely natural, while using it to heighten dramatic elements in the narrative.

Moving West

George Wilson tells Tom that he has lived at the garage too long and needs to move away. He plans to go West, taking Myrtle with him. The Wilsons have been in the 'valley of ashes' for eleven years. They have become fixed in that place, just as Gatsby's unsuccessful parents were stuck on their farm. Gatsby managed to moved away while still young, but George Wilson is older, poor and tired. His dream of a fresh start will not be realised.

Note that George Wilson's face looks 'green' in the sunlight (p. 117). Elsewhere in this novel the colour green is associated with natural freshness and growth, but in Wilson's case it suggests that he is unwell or that he is green with envy of Tom's wealth and power. Nick tells us that Wilson has been made ill by the shock of discovering that Myrtle has 'some sort of life apart from him in another world' (p. 118). He adds that Tom, for all his wealth and power, 'had made a parallel discovery less than an hour before' (p. 118) – that is, he had found out that Daisy had been seeing Gatsby.

A sense of purpose

In Chapter 4, Nick says that when he found out that Gatsby was driven by his intense love for Daisy, 'He came alive to me, delivered suddenly from the womb of his purposeless splendour' (p. 76). Gatsby has a sense of purpose which seems to be lacking in the lives of most of the characters in this novel. We might question whether his pursuit of Daisy is worthwhile; but in a world of drifters he does at least have a sense of direction in his life.

In the energy-sapping heat of Chapter 7, Daisy herself expresses a sense of purposeless drifting: '"What'll we do with ourselves this afternoon?'" cried Daisy, "and the day after that, and the next thirty years?"' (p. 113). The very wealthy Buchanans have all they need and are able to move from place to place, but they have no goals or dreams. So Daisy wonders how they will spend the rest of their lives.

Remember that these characters are still quite young. But Nick Carraway grows melancholy as he realises that this day is his thirtieth birthday: 'Thirty – the promise of a decade of loneliness, a thinning list of single men to know, a thinning brief-case of enthusiasm, thinning hair' (p. 129). Nick's dismal vision of life's diminishing potential contrasts markedly with his earlier statement of appreciation for Gatsby's 'heightened sensitivity to the promises of life' (p. 8).

Two-thirds of the way through this long chapter, Nick returns home to Long Island, with Tom, Jordan, Daisy and Gatsby. At this point he writes, 'So we drove on toward death through the cooling twilight' (p. 129). We may think he is referring to the inevitable passage of time, and that he is gloomily envisaging the end of life that awaits them all. The sentence fits in well with his melancholy musings on being thirty, and getting older every day. But after a brief pause in the text, like a skilful cut from one scene to another in a film, Nick refers to an inquest, and we discover that Myrtle Wilson has been killed. They were, in fact, driving towards the scene of her death.

The American West plays a significant part in this novel, even though it is set on the East coast. Horace Greeley (1811–72), editor of the *New York Tribune*, is credited with offering the famous advice 'Go West!' to Americans seeking opportunities for self-advancement. The phrase became a popular slogan, but westward movement was already firmly associated with the American dream of a fresh start or a new beginning.

Violence

There is a great deal of glamour and party-going in *The Great Gatsby*, but there is also a considerable amount of violence. Myrtle Wilson, a woman who is said to have 'tremendous vitality' (p. 131), has had her nose broken by Tom Buchanan, and now she is killed by a car driven by Daisy. Remember that earlier that day Myrtle had seen Tom driving the 'death car' (p. 131); she later ran into the road, desperate to speak with him. This is not a straightforward accident, but a terrible and unforeseen outcome of her affair with Tom.

Descriptions of violent action can seem melodramatic, or just repulsive. Note the skill with which Fitzgerald presents Myrtle's death indirectly, through the testimony of Michaelis and other bystanders. Nick was not present at the incident, of course. But, reporting what others saw, he still manages to convey the horrific impact of Myrtle's mutilated body: 'her left breast was swinging loose like a flap, and there was no need to listen for the heart beneath' (p. 131).

The Great Gatsby is a highly patterned literary work, interweaving key themes, significant words and recurrent images. This description of Myrtle's severed breast may remind us of 'the pap of life' from which, in Chapter 6, Gatsby is said to 'gulp down the incomparable milk of wonder' (p. 107). It also **foreshadows** the reference, in Chapter 9, to 'a fresh, green breast of the new world' (p. 171). Those are visionary images, but Myrtle's torn breast is physically real, and her heart is no longer beating.

Social mobility

Tom accuses Gatsby of being 'Mr Nobody from Nowhere' (p. 123). America has for a long time taken pride in being a place where there is social mobility, a land where people can make a fresh start and find success no matter what their background. But Tom Buchanan is saying that Gatsby is a social upstart and not to be trusted, because he doesn't have a well-established family background like his own.

Gatsby is a self-made man. Not just in terms of money – he has also made a whole new identity for himself. Tom, on the other hand, has inherited wealth and a lifestyle that recalls the Old World aristocracy. He has polo ponies and boasts of being 'the first man who ever made a stable out of a garage' (p. 113). Tom takes advantage of the conveniences that come with modern life, such as cars and telephones, but he wants to preserve a world of privilege. In converting a garage to a stable, he seems to be reversing the trend of history in which motor cars have irreversibly superseded horses when it comes to transport. But Tom's ponies are just for show, and remember that George Wilson, a poor working man, depends on his own garage for survival.

Class distinctions

At the start of his narration, Nick mentions a Carraway family tradition that 'we're descended from the Dukes of Buccleuch' (p. 8), although in fact the Carraways run a hardware business. Fitzgerald seems to be suggesting that, although America has made a break with Europe, it still idealises the lifestyle of the European upper classes.

Tom is a snob. He says that Gatsby was too poor and lower class to be a suitable lover for Daisy: 'I'll be damned if I see how you got within a mile of her unless you brought the groceries to the back door' (p. 125). In fact, Gatsby came into contact with Daisy while he was training for war service, and during the war his bravery led to promotion to the rank of major.

Tom also calls into question Gatsby's reputation as 'an Oxford man' (p. 122). Gatsby's response is honest. He went to that prestigious English university for only five months, being offered the opportunity because of his service as an officer in the army. Nick admires Gatsby's honesty at this point: 'I had one of those renewals of complete faith in him that I'd experienced before' (p. 123). Note however that in Chapter 8 we learn that, at the end of the war, Gatsby was desperate to return to America so he could be with Daisy; but 'some complication or misunderstanding sent him to Oxford instead' (p. 143).

Revision task 6: Understanding the Buchanans **A02**

Make notes on ways in which your understanding of Tom and Daisy Buchanan develops during this chapter. Pay particular attention to:

● How Daisy behaves with her daughter Pammy
● How Tom responds to Gatsby's love for Daisy

Key quotation: Mr Nobody from Nowhere **A02**

On page 123, Tom speaks dismissively of Gatsby as, 'Mr Nobody from Nowhere'.

Tom's description implies that Gatsby is socially unacceptable because he doesn't come from a well-established and wealthy family like his own. It also acknowledges that Gatsby's background is mysterious, and perhaps sinister. Tom's intention is to belittle this inexplicably wealthy man who is infatuated with Daisy. But is there something admirable in the way Gatsby has erased his past in order to become free to take on a new identity? Is that not what America itself has tried to achieve?

Further key quotations

● Gatsby says of Daisy: 'Her voice is full of money.' (p. 115)
● Daisy, regarding Gatsby: '"You resemble the advertisement of the man", she went on innocently. "You know the advertisement of the man –"' (p. 114)
● Tom, regarding Gatsby: 'I'll be damned if I see how you got within a mile of her unless you brought the groceries to the back door.' (p. 125)

A02 **PROGRESS BOOSTER**

Although Nick Carraway is still narrating, this chapter makes extensive use of **dialogue** amongst the characters. Pay close attention to the ways in which dialogue, which may seem no more than small-talk, sheds light on the characters speaking. Tom speaks in a way that has a very different effect to the way Jordan speaks, for example. What they say may be trivial, but Fitzgerald is still developing our understanding of their characters.

A03 **KEY CONTEXT**

Fitzgerald was born in the Midwest. His family had largely Irish ancestry. One of his distant American relatives, Francis Scott Key (1779–1843), wrote the American national anthem, 'The Star-Spangled Banner'. Matthew J. Bruccoli's biography *Some Sort of Epic Grandeur: The Life of F. Scott Fitzgerald* (University of South Carolina Press, 2002) provides illuminating background information on the author of *The Great Gatsby*.

CHAPTER 8

Summary

- After a sleepless night, Nick visits Gatsby as dawn approaches. Gatsby talks of his past, and of his love for Daisy, described as 'the following of a grail' (p. 142).
- Gatsby's gardener postpones draining the swimming pool, as Gatsby wants to use it.
- At noon, at work, Nick receives a call from Jordan Baker.
- George Wilson, grief-stricken at Myrtle's death, mistakes the eyes of Doctor T. J. Eckleburg on an advertising hoarding for the eyes of an all-seeing God.
- Wilson searches for the owner of the yellow car that killed his wife. He is directed to Gatsby, finds him floating in his swimming pool, and kills him. He then shoots himself.

Analysis

Ashes to ashes, dust to dust

Inside Gatsby's mansion Nick notices that now 'there was an inexplicable amount of dust everywhere' (p. 140). The word 'dust' should remind us of the description in Chapter 2 of George Wilson's home, in the valley of ashes, where 'a white ashen dust' covers everything (p. 28). Nick, Gatsby's neighbour, keeps Gatsby company at this difficult time; and Michaelis tries to look after his neighbour, George Wilson. Gatsby and Wilson are otherwise friendless men. At the end of this chapter, their separate lives converge, and both men die.

Note that in Chapter 1 Nick writes of the 'foul dust' that floated in the wake of Gatsby's dreams (p. 8). Note also that in Chapter 9 Tom, talking to Nick about Gatsby, says 'He threw dust into your eyes just like he did in Daisy's, but he was a tough one' (p. 169). Tom is alluding to the magic dust found in various legends and old stories which, when sprinkled in the eyes, induces sleep or dreams. But by this point in the novel, the association of dust and ashes with death has been firmly implanted in our minds.

Identity

It is shortly before Gatsby's death that Nick actually finds out the truth about him. He tells us that '"Jay Gatsby" had broken up like glass against Tom's hard malice' (p. 141). The new identity taken on by young James Gatz has been shattered, and it is at this point that Gatsby lets Nick into the secret of his life-changing meetings with Dan Cody and with Daisy Fay.

Nick has already told us the story of Gatsby's life on Cody's yacht. He has saved the details about Gatsby's early encounters with Daisy until now. Nick's narration is skilfully structured in order to sustain a sense of mystery, while gradually revealing more and more about the reality behind Gatsby's image.

Mistaken identity plays a key role in the later chapters of this novel. Myrtle thinks that Tom, rather than Daisy, is driving Gatsby's car. George Wilson believes that Gatsby has killed his wife, and in his grief he mistakes the eyes of Doctor T. J. Eckleburg on an advertising hoarding for the eyes of an all-seeing God.

KEY CONTEXT **A03**

The dustiness of the 'valley of ashes' is a **realistic** detail, but it also lends itself to a more figurative interpretation. Genesis, the first book of the Bible, reminds its readers: 'Dust thou art, and unto dust thou shalt return.' That image of human mortality is echoed in the well-known phrase from the Anglican burial service, 'Ashes to ashes, dust to dust'. If we recognise this allusion it may be seen to **foreshadow** the death of Myrtle Wilson.

Class

In Chapter 7, Tom snobbishly says to Gatsby, 'I'll be damned if I see how you got within a mile of her unless you brought the groceries to the back door' (p. 125). It is a spiteful comment, but it has an element of truth. Gatsby had met people of Daisy's social class before, 'but always with indiscernible barbed wire between' (p. 141). This 'barbed wire', figuratively keeping a distance between young Gatsby and the social elite, is a powerfully suggestive **metaphor**, given the use of barbed wire during the recent war in Europe.

Gatsby's sense of Daisy's social superiority, her wealth and 'comfortable family' (p. 142), makes explicit the class divisions within American society: 'Gatsby was overwhelmingly aware of the youth and mystery that wealth imprisons and preserves, of the freshness of many clothes, and of Daisy, gleaming like silver, safe and proud above the hot struggles of the poor' (p. 142). Equal opportunity is no longer a reality for Americans in the 1920s.

Daisy's family home in Louisville is described as a place that is at once 'cool' and 'radiant', a house that has 'a ripe mystery about it' (p. 141). In his own mansion, Gatsby has sought to capture that same sense of coolness, radiance and mystery, to make it attractive for Daisy.

The knight in the pink suit

Daisy became Gatsby's 'grail' (p. 142), the sacred object of his quest. His total devotion is reminiscent of the unswerving loyalty shown by knights in the medieval tales of King Arthur and his court. Gatsby is presented as a chivalrous hero whose shining armour takes the form of immaculate suits and shirts, whose trusty steed is his expensive automobile. Once again Old World values cast their long shadow across modern American realities.

Study focus: Descriptive technique **A02**

Note the indirect way in which Fitzgerald presents Gatsby's death. A less skilful novelist might have resorted to melodramatic description. But Nick Carraway, our **narrator**, was not present to witness the killing at first hand, and the death of the novel's central character is rendered through shots reportedly heard by Gatsby's chauffeur. Look carefully at the steady build-up to this key incident. The pacing of **dialogue** between the characters is particularly worthy of attention.

Home sweet home

Nick observes that Gatsby 'must have felt that he had lost the old warm world, paid a high price for living too long with a single dream' (p. 153). The 'old' world referred to here is not Europe but the Midwest, where Gatsby grew up. There is a verbal echo at this point of Nick's earlier remark that after the war the Midwest was no longer for him 'the warm centre of the world' (p. 9). Nick seems to miss the womb-like security of his childhood home. He has, of course, returned there in order to write his account of Gatsby's life.

Gatsby made a deliberate break with the past and has tried to make a fresh start. But by the end of his life, Nick suggests, this 'new world' of Gatsby's own making has become a strange and unsettling place, lit by 'raw' sunlight: 'A new world, material without being real, where poor ghosts, breathing dreams like air, drifted fortuitously about … like that ashen, fantastic figure gliding toward him through the amorphous trees' (pp. 153–4). That figure belongs to George Wilson, who is about to kill Jay Gatsby.

A03 **KEY CONTEXT**

By describing Daisy as Gatsby's 'grail' Fitzgerald connects this modern novel to the medieval European tradition of chivalric quest. The Holy Grail was the cup from which Jesus Christ drank at the Last Supper. It was used by Joseph of Arimathea to catch Christ's blood during the Crucifixion. The quest for the Grail became a major **narrative** element in legends of King Arthur and his court, found notably in *Le Morte d'Arthur* [The Death of Arthur] (1485) by Sir Thomas Malory (1405–71). Sir Galahad was the knight who led the quest for this sacred vessel.

CHAPTER 9

Summary

- Nick makes the arrangements for Gatsby's funeral.
- The Buchanans have left New York, leaving no contact address.
- Nick visits Meyer Wolfshiem, who says he is unable to attend the funeral.
- One of the few mourners present is Henry C. Gatz, who has travelled from the Midwest, after reading of Gatsby's death in a Chicago newspaper. He speaks with pride of his son's attainments.
- Later in the year, Nick bumps into Tom Buchanan, who admits telling George Wilson that it was Gatsby's car which killed Myrtle.
- The novel ends with Nick contemplating the empty mansion, and pondering the significance of Gatsby's story.

Analysis

The scene of the crime

Note the vocabulary Nick uses when describing the aftermath of Gatsby's murder. The words 'adventitious' (meaning incidental) and 'pasquinade' (meaning a lampoon or parody) leap out as unfamiliar words. Such vocabulary seems to have been chosen to keep us at a distance from the crime scene.

You might expect that this description of a crime scene, complete with police investigators and news reporters, would include a degree of sensationalism. But there is a kind of protective formality in Nick's use of such words, as though he wants to shield his neighbour from the effects of gossip and lurid reporting. We are not led to feel like onlookers, gawping at the scene; rather, we are made aware of the presence of Nick, our careful **narrator**.

Friends and neighbours

In this final chapter, Nick emphasises Gatsby's isolation. After hosting all those lavish parties, it turns out that he was essentially alone all the time. Nick has only known Gatsby for three months at the time of his death, yet it is left to him to arrange the funeral. Owl Eyes attends the ceremony, yet he never really knew Gatsby at all. His presence seems random, and that makes Gatsby's aloneness seem still more complete.

We might conclude that Gatsby deserved to be so isolated; it is the price he paid for 'living too long with a single dream' (p. 153). Up to this point we have been led to understand that Gatsby totally erased his past, left his parents behind and had no further contact with them. But Nick now reveals that Gatsby has in fact sent his father, Henry C. Gatz, a photograph of his mansion. He has, moreover, visited his father and bought him a house too. Henry C. Gatz is proud of his son and says, 'ever since he made a success he was very generous with me' (p. 164).

Is this true, or is the old man deluding himself? Henry C. Gatz seems an honest man, whose word we ought to trust. The well-worn photograph he carries also suggests that he is telling the truth. Remember that ever since this funeral Nick has been aware of Gatz's claim that his son kept in touch and was good to him. Yet all through the narration so far he has led us to believe that Gatsby simply turned his back on his parents. Introducing this sense that the break with his past wasn't total, Nick now makes Gatsby seem more human, less aloof and more deserving of his and our own sympathy.

Revision task 7: The human side of Gatsby
A02

It could be argued that the presence of Henry C. Gatz at his son's funeral makes Jay Gatsby seem more human.

Make notes reflecting upon ways in which Fitzgerald's characterisation of Henry C. Gatz modifies your perception of Gatsby and of other characters in the novel.

A story of the West

We have noticed how, from the outset, this novel located in New York, on America's East coast, has made extensive use of the American West's long association with new beginnings and unlimited potential. Nick now talks of growing up in the Midwest, not on the West coast but in the physical heart of the American republic. He remembers going home from school and from college, and associates the Middle West with 'the thrilling returning trains of my youth' (p. 167). As a boy and young man, he found the westward journey exhilarating, but note that he was returning to the bosom of his family, rather than heading out for some unexplored and unsettled wilderness.

At this point he realises that 'this has been a story of the West, after all' (p. 167). The European settlement of America started on the East coast and moved steadily across the continent to the West coast. But the characters in this book have moved in the opposite direction – from America's cosy Middle to its exciting and energetic East – and Nick suggests that their solid, comfortable upbringing didn't prepare them for the more dynamic and competitive conditions of life in New York.

Progress booster: The power of vision
A02

After Gatsby's death, Nick says that life in the East seemed to be 'distorted beyond my eyes' power of correction' (p. 167). Vision is an important theme in *The Great Gatsby*. This theme covers issues ranging from the difficulty of making a clear-sighted interpretation of events to the power of seeing beyond immediate circumstances, using the visionary capacity of hope and imagination. Does Nick really prefer to see things as they are? Or would he prefer to see things as they might become?

Study focus: A shared deficiency
A02

Nick tells us that he 'began to have a feeling of defiance, of scornful solidarity between Gatsby and me against them all' (p. 157). Ten pages later, however, he identifies himself not just with Gatsby, but also with Tom, Daisy and Jordan. They are all Midwesterners, and 'perhaps had some deficiency in common which made us subtly unadaptable to Eastern life' (p. 167). Nick's narration is the means by which we get to know all these characters. But can you identify attitudes or characteristics he shares with all four?

A03 **KEY CONTEXT**

Nick compares West Egg after Gatsby's death to 'a night scene by El Greco' (p. 167). El Greco (1541–1614) was a Spanish painter of religious scenes whose figures tended to seem elongated and oddly distorted. Think carefully about the role played in this novel by distorted vision. Gatsby's view of Daisy may seem out of proportion to her actual merits; but could the same be said about Nick's view of Gatsby?

EXTRACT ANALYSIS

Chapter 9, pp. 170–2

This passage is pervaded by a sense of things coming to an end; it has an air of finality. The word 'last' occurs three times on p. 171. The party is over in a literal and a **metaphorical** sense, and Nick is preparing to leave the bustling, energetic East for the quiet, reflective Midwest. But his departure is followed by a new beginning. Two years after returning home, Nick will write this account, living through the experiences of that summer once again in his memory and imagination, as he carefully composes his book. In a sense, Nick has brought Jay Gatsby, his former neighbour, back to life through the preceding pages, and has transformed himself; this worker in the world of finance has become a creative writer of prose.

Light plays an important role throughout *The Great Gatsby*: the green light at the end of Daisy's dock; the blaze of electric lighting at Gatsby's parties; the glare of the hot sun in Chapter 7. Fitzgerald understood well how our perception of things can change according to changes in the light, and in *The Great Gatsby* he makes light itself an important component in the **narrative**. The end of the novel is illuminated by moonlight. The world seen by moonlight can appear very different to the brightly lit world of daytime, and it is fitting that the closing pages of *The Great Gatsby* should be bathed in this more mysterious kind of light. Fitzgerald's book mixes **realism** with **romance**.

The term 'romance' is often used to indicate a love story. Fitzgerald's book is certainly that. But romance has a more specialised meaning, defined helpfully by an earlier American writer, Nathaniel Hawthorne (1804–64). In 'The Custom-House', an introductory essay to his own romance *The Scarlet Letter* (1850), Hawthorne wrote:

> Moonlight, in a familiar room, falling so white upon the carpet, and showing all its figures so distinctly, – making every object so minutely visible, yet so unlike a morning or noontide visibility, – is a medium the most suitable for a romance-writer to get acquainted with his illusive guests … the floor of our familiar room has become a neutral territory, somewhere between the real world and fairy-land, where the Actual and the Imaginary may meet, and each imbue itself with the nature of the other.

This classic passage may help you to understand more fully the kind of book that Fitzgerald has written. The world of romance, located 'somewhere between the real world and fairy-land', is a suitable place to find Jay Gatsby, who in Chapter 6 is said to believe that 'the rock of the world was founded securely on a fairy's wing' (p. 96).

KEY CONNECTION **A04**

Realism and romance are combined with considerable subtlety in *The Great Gatsby*. Mark Twain's characters Huck Finn and Tom Sawyer, in *The Adventures of Huckleberry Finn* (1884), respectively represent a kind of realism and a crude form of romance, in their ways of looking at the world. Huck's realism increasingly takes on an ethical dimension, responding to the needs and feelings of others, whereas Tom Sawyer's flights of fancy tend to be little more than irresponsible escapism.

In the aftermath of Gatsby's death, the moon illuminates an obscene word that some boy has written on one of the steps of Gatsby's mansion. Nick erases the scrawl, already guarding Jay Gatsby's memory against other people's words. Nick also makes reference in this passage to a taxi driver, who pauses as he passes Gatsby's house in order to share with passengers his own version of events. The taxi driver knows that people tend to love gossip, especially if it has an element of scandal. Myrtle Wilson loved to read such stories in the magazine *Town Tattle*. Nick clearly wants to prevent that kind of tattle after Gatsby's death, and he writes his book caringly, to set the record straight.

Initially, Fitzgerald placed the reference to Dutch sailors encountering the New World at the end of Chapter 1, but in the course of writing this novel he shifted it to the end, where it provides a resonant and memorable conclusion.

Fitzgerald suggests that America (for Old World settlers, not for the Native Americans they removed or displaced) was founded on 'a transitory enchanted moment' when a newly arrived European came 'face to face for the last time in history with something commensurate to his capacity for wonder' (p. 171). America is a physical place; yet its history has been fuelled by dreams. Is Fitzgerald suggesting that the dreams upon which the American republic was founded have been betrayed by its historical reality? Is he suggesting that America, like Gatsby's house after his death, now appears to be 'a huge incoherent failure' (p. 171)?

The final paragraphs strongly convey the irreversible passing of time. The Dutch sailors, who arrived on this coast and were astonished at what they found, are long gone. The trees that once grew there have made way for Gatsby's house, and now Gatsby himself has gone. Does America remain a land of promise, or has its potential been exhausted? The narrative focus narrows from 'the fresh, green breast of the new world' to 'the green light' at the end of the Buchanans' dock (p. 171). Nick contemplates the failure of Gatsby's dream, and identifies the green light with 'the orgastic future that year by year recedes before us' (p. 171). 'Orgastic' is another example of Nick's taste for obscure words. It looks like 'orgiastic', meaning riotous or indulgent, and might seem to refer back to the wild parties that Gatsby hosted.

But when his editor, Maxwell Perkins, queried the word 'orgastic', F. Scott Fitzgerald explained that it was an adjective from 'orgasm', an alternative version of orgasmic, and that it was intended to express a state of ecstasy. Orgasm, as a culminating moment of sexual excitement, suggests intense experience which seems to stand outside the flow of historical time. Gatsby's dream of Daisy seems to have been not just erotic, but ecstatic – he was less concerned with her physical reality, than with clinging on to that feeling of standing outside of historical time that he experienced at the moment of falling in love with her.

Falling in love seems to have made Gatsby feel immortal. Now, however, he is dead, and his story is told by Nick, who at thirty is very conscious of growing older. Remember that James Gatz 'invented just the sort of Jay Gatsby that a seventeen-year-old boy would be likely to invent, and to this conception he was faithful to the end' (p. 95). Gatsby was imagined by a boy on the verge of becoming an adult. Adulthood, however, teaches us that we are not immortal, that we cannot live forever in moments of intensity and enchantment. Time passes: 'So we beat on, boats against the current, borne back ceaselessly into the past' (p. 172).

  KEY INTERPRETATION

An eco-critical reading of *The Great Gatsby* might compare the pristine natural environment, figuratively represented by the 'fresh, green breast of the new world' (p. 171), with the 'valley of ashes' in which the Wilsons struggle to make a living. Industrialisation and urban settlement might, in light of that contrast, be regarded as a betrayal of America's potential as a New World. Myrtle's death in a car accident might be interpreted as symptomatic of a damaging imbalance in the relationship between nature and human society.

PROGRESS CHECK

Section One: Check your understanding

These tasks will help you to evaluate your knowledge and skills level in this particular area.

1. Can Nick Carraway be regarded as a reliable **narrator**? Make a table of reasons for and against.

2. Write a paragraph outlining your understanding of the relationship between Nick and Daisy.

3. List five instances of violent action in *The Great Gatsby* and comment briefly upon the significance of each.

4. In your view is Gatsby motivated more by a passion for his own self-image than by love for Daisy? List four or five reasons that support your viewpoint.

5. What is the significance of new beginnings in this novel? Write a paragraph outlining your thoughts.

6. How is the Jazz Age reflected in the action of the novel? Write a paragraph summarising your thoughts.

7. List four actual events in American history that feature in the **narrative**, and briefly describe the significance of each in relation to the story.

8. List four to five key moments in the narrative that shed light on the character of Jay Gatsby.

9. What do you find striking about the way Fitzgerald presents Gatsby's death? List three or four key aspects of the way that scene is written.

10. What does Nick's writing style tell us about his character? Write a paragraph discussing this idea.

11. What is the narrative function of parties in this novel? Write a couple of paragraphs detailing your ideas.

12. What is the significance of names in *The Great Gatsby*? Write down four or five names and the significance of each.

13. List four or five occasions in the narrative where memory plays a significant role. Briefly describe that role.

14. How is the impact of the First World War felt in this novel? List and briefly describe three or four details.

15. What is the significance of Gatsby's funeral? Write a paragraph exploring this.

16. List four to five key moments in the narrative that shed light on the character of Daisy Buchanan.

17. Make a table contrasting the character of the American Midwest and of New York, as they are depicted in the novel, in order to shed light on Nick's assertion that 'this has been a story of the West, after all' (p. 167).

18. What is the significance of the motor car in *The Great Gatsby*? Write a paragraph discussing your viewpoint.

19. Identify three or four journeys undertaken or referred to in the narrative and briefly explain the significance of each.

20. Write a paragraph outlining how you see the relationship between Fitzgerald as author of the novel and Nick as its narrator.

Section Two: Working towards the exam

Below are five tasks which require longer, more developed answers. In each case, read the question carefully, select the key areas you need to address, and plan an essay of six or seven points. Write a first draft, giving yourself an hour to do so. Make sure you include supporting evidence for each point, including quotations.

1. '*The Great Gatsby* is an exploration of the relationship between fact and fiction.' Discuss.

2. Consider the role of memory in this novel.

3. How far can Nick be seen as a kind of amateur detective writing an account of the circumstances surrounding a murder?

4. How far do you agree with the contention that '*The Great Gatsby* is a novel that lacks a moral centre'?

5. How is the novel's concern with the passage of time reflected in its narrative structure?

Progress check (rate your understanding on a level of 1 – low, to 5 – high)	1	2	3	4	5
The significance of particular events and how they relate to each other					
How the major and minor characters contribute to the action					
How Fitzgerald uses the device of the narrator					
How Fitzgerald structures the narrative					
The final outcome of the story and how this affects our view of the protagonist and the narrator					

CHARACTERS

Jay Gatsby

Who is Jay Gatsby?

- A wealthy, glamorous and mysterious figure, who throws lavish parties at his mansion in Long Island, New York.
- A Midwestern youth called James Gatz, who has reinvented himself.
- A man who seems to embody idealistic love, but in fact has close connections with the criminal underworld.

Nick Carraway's neighbour

Jay Gatsby is Nick Carraway's neighbour, in West Egg village, Long Island. Nick, our **narrator**, lives in a small house; Gatsby has a huge mansion set in an enormous garden. He is attended by servants, owns expensive cars, motorboats and a hydroplane. Gatsby regularly throws lavish parties, with fine food and drink and music for dancing.

Before Nick meets Gatsby he imagines him to be 'a florid and corpulent person in his middle years' (p. 50). In fact, he is a year or two over thirty, sun-tanned and handsome with short hair, well groomed and immaculately dressed. Although he is an extravagantly generous host, he drinks very little and keeps himself apart, almost an onlooker at his own parties.

Mr Nobody from Nowhere

Gatsby's background is a mystery. Tom Buchanan calls him 'Mr Nobody from Nowhere' (p. 123). Because not much is known about Gatsby, there is a lot of gossip about him. He is said to have attended Oxford University. A common rumour suggests that he has killed a man. There is also speculation that he was a German spy, working for the enemy during the First World War, and that he is related to the German ruler Kaiser Wilhelm II. These rumours suggest, perhaps, that Gatsby's physical appearance is Germanic. Nick has discovered some details of Gatsby's actual background, and as he narrates this story he gradually discloses more and more of the facts that lie behind Gatsby's image as a man of mystery.

Study focus: Gatsby's greatness

The title *The Great Gatsby* prepares us, as readers, for the story of an exceptional man. Think carefully about elements of his story that show Gatsby to be in some sense 'great'. Pay attention too to character flaws that suggest just the opposite of 'greatness'. Remember that Nick, our narrator, is the lens through which we see Gatsby. Is it a distorting lens or can we trust the image of Gatsby that eventually appears within Nick's account? What are we to make of Nick's assessment that 'Gatsby turned out all right at the end' (p. 8)?

From Gatz to Gatsby

James Gatz grew up in North Dakota, in America's Midwest, the son of unsuccessful farm people. At seventeen he changed his name to Jay Gatsby. As a boy he explored the shores of Lake Superior, becoming physically fit and getting to know the natural world in that area. This enabled him to warn Dan Cody that his yacht was moored in a potentially dangerous place. Cody, who had grown rich prospecting for precious metals, became a kind of surrogate father for Gatsby. Following Cody's death, Gatsby became involved with the gambler Meyer Wolfshiem, a shady and sinister figure from the underworld of organised crime. Wolfshiem not only describes Gatsby as 'a perfect gentleman' and 'a man of fine breeding', but he suggests that he is 'the kind of man you'd like to take home and introduce to your mother and sister' (p. 70). Gatsby clearly has charm, an element of charisma. Nick notices especially that he has 'one of those rare smiles with a quality of eternal reassurance in it' (p. 49).

Making Gatsby great

Gatsby takes great pains to present himself as a gentleman and a man of breeding. He owns a Rolls-Royce car and has his clothes bought at expensive shops in London. He habitually uses the term 'old sport', a phrase intended to make him seem upper class. Gatsby is acting out a role, and Nick indicates that he is trying a little too hard, that his 'elaborate formality of speech just missed being absurd' (p. 49). In his mansion, Gatsby has a library with English oak panelling, designed to resemble one you might find in an Oxford college. The character Owl Eyes, who doesn't really know Gatsby at all, is hugely impressed by the **realistic** appearance of the library, although he notes that the pages of the books remain uncut, and are unread. Gatsby aims to project the image of an Old World aristocrat. He actually comes across as an extravagant, yet very thorough, New World showman.

The war

We are told that Gatsby 'did extraordinarily well in the war' (p. 143). His brave conduct during the conflict resulted in promotion to the rank of major. This enhanced his social status, and seems to have made it easier for him to make useful connections. A scheme that enabled American officers to attend European universities also led to him spending five months at Oxford.

Seen from another angle, however, the war was disastrous for Gatsby. As a young lieutenant, before leaving to fight in France, he met Daisy Fay in Louisville, Kentucky and fell head over heels in love. During his absence overseas Daisy met and married Tom Buchanan. The conduct of Gatsby's life from that moment had a single goal – to win back Daisy's love and to take her away from her husband. The intensity of that obsession separates Gatsby from the crowd; he is a man driven by desire, and his life has purpose. But that obsession leads to his downfall.

Image and reality

Gatsby presents himself as a wealthy American who doesn't need to work. But, as Nick remarks, young men didn't just 'drift coolly out of nowhere and buy a palace on Long Island Sound' (p. 50). In three years, Gatsby had made the money to buy this luxurious mansion. He did so through the criminal activity of bootlegging, supplying alcoholic drink illegally. His close involvement with Wolfshiem suggests that he has taken part in other illicit activities. Gatsby acts out the role of a sophisticated man of the world, yet when he meets Daisy again after five years apart he is overcome with embarrassment and nervousness; Nick actually tells him, 'You're acting like a little boy' (p. 85). The fact is, when James Gatz changed his name 'he invented just the sort of Jay Gatsby that a seventeen-year-old boy would be likely to invent, and to this conception he was faithful to the end' (p. 95).

A03 KEY CONTEXT

Owl Eyes compares Gatsby to David Belasco (1853–1931), a New York theatre producer renowned for paying close attention to realistic details on the stage. Belasco is said to have been so painstaking that once when he needed a restaurant setting he bought a real one and had it moved to the theatre and reassembled on stage. He was also renowned for his spectacular use of new lighting techniques.

A02 KEY QUOTATION

On page 95, Nick says: 'So he invented just the sort of Jay Gatsby that a seventeen-year-old boy would be likely to invent.'

James Gatz transformed himself into Jay Gatsby at a time in his life when experience of the world had not yet placed limits on his imagination. But the energy of his youthful vision lacked clarity of purpose. It remained a wild dream, attaching itself to Daisy as an object of desire. Nick admires the fact that 'to this conception he was faithful to the end' (p. 95), yet he is aware of the tragic consequences.

Nick Carraway

Who is Nick?

- The **narrator** of *The Great Gatsby*.
- Daisy's second cousin once removed, and Gatsby's next-door neighbour.
- A worker in the world of finance, who returns to the Midwest and becomes a writer.

The Midwest and the wider world

Nick Carraway's family run a hardware business and have become well-to-do. Nick grew up in a Midwestern city. He has returned there after working in finance in New York City, on the East coast. Before entering the financial world, Nick had graduated from Yale University. He had also served in the American army, in France, in the First World War.

A literary man

At the start of his **narrative**, Nick tells us that he and his father have always been 'unusually communicative in a reserved way' (p. 7). The meaning of this phrase seems to be that, although they may not say much , their words are carefully chosen and rich in implication. That seems a good basis for his ambition to become a writer.

Nick tells us that he was 'rather literary in college' (p. 10). Now he is the narrator of this story, as well as a character in it. In fact, he tells us he is actually writing the book we are reading. So we come to know Nick's character in part through his literary style and his use of language.

Nick is well educated, and he occasionally uses obscure words. It is surprising, perhaps, that a worker in finance, from a family in the hardware business, should have such a poetic and lyrical style. Nick presents himself as a dull and ordinary individual, but his writing discloses a passionate and imaginative nature, despite his outwardly reserved demeanour.

Progress booster: Is Nick a man you can trust?

Consider the range of possible ways you can interpret Nick's narration. He tells us that his quiet demeanour has led others to confide in him, to share their 'intimate revelations' (p. 7). Other young men have put their trust in his tact and tolerance, and as a consequence he has become aware of secret stories and hidden truths.

This may help to explain why he is so interested in Jay Gatsby, whose polished and carefully maintained appearance concealed so much. But as he reveals the truth about Gatsby, Nick also sheds light on aspects of his own character, and at times our perception of him may not fit comfortably with what he says openly about himself. Is Nick a reliable narrator, a man we can trust? Or does his own hidden truth shape and colour the way he tells this tale? Is Jay Gatsby a convenient front for the secret story of Nick Carraway?

Melancholy

Nick seems to find the world a profoundly sad place, and he has the verbal skills to express that: 'At the enchanted metropolitan twilight I felt a haunting loneliness sometimes, and felt it in others' (p. 57). He gets melancholy when he contemplates growing old. Although only thirty, he foresees a bleak future, 'the promise of a decade of loneliness, a thinning list of single men to know, a thinning brief-case of enthusiasm, thinning hair' (p. 129).

Can we take such expressions of intense sadness at face value? Perhaps his experience of the war has left him feeling prematurely old and pessimistic. Or maybe there is an element of self-dramatisation in these melancholy statements.

Unlucky in love?

Tom and Daisy tell Nick that they have heard rumours of his engagement to 'a girl out West'. Nick responds, within his narrative, with characteristic reserve: 'Of course I knew what they were referring to, but I wasn't even vaguely engaged' (p. 24). We might be tempted to disregard the gossip surrounding this relationship, but at the close of Chapter 3 Nick refers to it as 'that tangle back home' and reveals that he has been writing once a week to that young woman, ending each letter, 'Love, Nick' (p. 59). What is Nick concealing from us?

Our suspicion that passionate undercurrents may run beneath the calm image that Nick projects is heightened by his surprising declaration: 'I liked to walk up Fifth Avenue and pick out romantic women from the crowd and imagine that in a few minutes I was going to enter into their lives, and no one would ever know or disapprove' (p. 57). Not only does Nick have a fantasy life that seems at odds with his cool exterior, but he also seems to fear public disapproval of his love affairs. What events and circumstances in Nick's life might lurk behind this unexpected revelation?

A careless driver

Towards the end of the novel, Jordan Baker tells Nick that he is a bad driver. She is alluding to a conversation reported on p. 59, in which he remarks that accidents occur when one careless driver meets another. 'I thought you were rather an honest, straightforward person' (p. 168), she complains. Whatever relationship has existed between these characters has now come to an end, and Jordan presents it in dramatic terms as a car crash. Nick does not share with us details of their affair, but it had clearly developed beyond a passing friendship. If Jordan has not found Nick to be honest or straightforward, can we as readers sustain our trust in all he has told us in the preceding narrative?

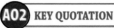

Study focus: Reserving judgements

At the start of the book, Nick tells us, 'I'm inclined to reserve all judgements.' He then adds, 'Reserving judgements is a matter of infinite hope' (p. 7). This is a quotation that is worth bearing in mind as you follow his narration. Nick is attracted to Gatsby's 'extraordinary gift for hope' (p. 8), but is Gatsby a worthy model to follow? Ask yourself what Nick might be hoping for.

Gatsby's belief in the possibility of regaining Daisy's love seems rather different from the kind of hope you experience when you hold back from passing judgement on someone or something.

A02 KEY QUOTATION

On page 57, Nick confides: 'I liked to walk up Fifth Avenue and pick out romantic women from the crowd and imagine that in a few minutes I was going to enter into their lives, and no one would ever know or disapprove.'

This revealing detail shows Nick's imagination at work in an everyday situation. He speaks of 'romantic women', but is projecting his own 'romantic' fantasies onto women whose appearance attracts him. Is the Jay Gatsby we see in the novel comparably a projection of Nick's romantic imagination? Is Nick, our narrator, more at home with fantasy than reality?

Daisy Buchanan (née Fay)

Who is Daisy?

- Nick Carraway's second cousin once removed.
- Tom Buchanan's wife.
- The woman Jay Gatsby loves.

The most popular girl in Louisville

Daisy Fay grew up in a wealthy family in Louisville, Kentucky, in the American Midwest. Gatsby met her there, when as a young military officer he was stationed at Camp Taylor, a nearby army base. Jordan Baker says that Daisy, who dressed in white and drove a white car, was 'by far the most popular of all the young girls in Louisville' (pp. 72–3). She is also said to have been popular in Chicago, after her marriage to Tom Buchanan. Yet, at the time of the novel's action, Daisy's social life seems rather limited, even dull, despite her wealth.

Daisy's voice

Daisy, who has 'dark shining hair' (p. 143), shares her name with a flower and there is a clear implication that physical delicacy is part of her allure. Nick recognises her attractiveness: 'Her face was sad and lovely with bright things in it … but there was an excitement in her voice that men who had cared for her found difficult to forget' (p. 14). How does Nick know this? Is he perhaps one of those men who has cared for her? Might a romantic fantasy of his own lie at the heart of Nick's interest in Jay Gatsby's obsessive pursuit of Daisy?

From the **dialogue** within this novel, Daisy's conversation appears to lack wit or sparkle and only occasional flashes of excitement relieve her general tone of boredom. But her voice clearly retains its seductive appeal, communicating far more than her words do. Nick responds to 'its fluctuating, feverish warmth' (p. 93). He tells us that when Gatsby had visited her, a few days after their first meeting in Louisville, she had a cold which 'made her voice huskier and more charming than ever' (p. 142), and when Daisy finally attends one of Gatsby's parties and begins to sing along with the music, Nick comments on her 'husky, rhythmic whisper' (p. 104).

Daisy's wealth

Note that Gatsby observes, 'Her voice is full of money' (p. 115). This blunt statement should alert us to the fact that since their first encounter in Louisville, Daisy's appeal for Gatsby has been laden with associations of social status and 'of the youth and mystery that wealth imprisons and preserves' (p. 142). Remember that Gatsby 'knew women early' (p. 95). Even before he lived on Dan Cody's yacht he seems to have had numerous physical relationships with women and he was worldly, in that sense. But Daisy 'was the first "nice" girl he had ever known' (p. 141).

Fay, Daisy's maiden name, suggests that she might have had Irish ancestry, but 'fay' is also an old English word for fairy. Gatsby obviously falls under her spell, but the enchantment he feels is in keeping with the life he has led with the prospector Dan Cody. Gatsby is aware of Daisy 'gleaming like silver, safe and proud above the hot struggles of the poor' (p. 142). She exists for him not simply as a physical presence, but as an embodiment of a way of life, given form also in 'her rich house' (p. 142). Does Gatsby really love Daisy? Or does he love something that she represents?

KEY CONTEXT **A03**

Daisy's maiden name, Fay, suggests Irish ancestry. Fitzgerald's own mother, Mary McQuillan, was the daughter of an Irish-American immigrant who became a wealthy wholesale grocer after fleeing the threat of starvation during the terrible famine that ravaged Ireland while under British rule, between 1845 and 1852.

Daisy and romance

When Nick visits Daisy in Chapter 1 he finds her sitting with Jordan upon an enormous couch: 'They were both in white, and their dresses were rippling and fluttering as if they had just been blown back in after a short flight around the house.' This is not the flight of two fairy-like creatures, however; Nick is comparing the couch on which they are perched with 'an anchored balloon' (p. 13), of the hot-air inflated kind that enables human beings to fly.

This strange and striking image may refer to a definition of the literary genre of **romance** offered by Henry James (1843–1916), an American writer much admired by Fitzgerald. In a retrospective preface he wrote in 1907 for his novel *The American* (1877), James wrote of the 'balloon of experience', and suggested that the writer of romance manages, without readers knowing, to cut the rope that anchors this balloon to the earth, setting it adrift, buoyed up by imagination. Fitzgerald may be suggesting that Daisy has a tendency to float in the realms of romance rather than being firmly grounded in **realism**.

Such an interpretation might be supported by reference to the moment when Daisy fancifully compares Nick to a rose (p. 19), or when she suggests that the bird singing on their lawn is a nightingale which has arrived from Europe on an ocean liner (p. 20). Rather than confirming that Daisy is imaginative, these images appear second-hand, worn-out and rather ridiculous. Her lack of an imagination that can engage constructively and productively with the world around her seems to be encapsulated in her helpless question 'What do people plan?' (p. 17).

Daisy as a mother

Daisy, who is in her early twenties, has a three-year-old daughter, named Pammy. The child is looked after by a nanny, and during the one scene where we see mother and daughter together Daisy's response to Pammy seems shallow and inadequate.

A01

Study focus: A beautiful little fool

Thinking about her daughter Pammy's future, Daisy says, 'that's the best thing a girl can be in this world, a beautiful little fool' (p. 22). Does that description fit Daisy's character? Has she lived up to her own ideal? Or are there respects in which Daisy seems worthy of Gatsby's devotion? Think carefully about the nature of her attraction for him.

A02

Key quotation: Daisy Buchanan

On page 22 Daisy says, 'I've been everywhere and seen everything and done everything'.

Daisy belongs to a privileged social class, and this statement reflects the easy mobility of her lifestyle. Unlike Gatsby's parents, scraping a living on their farm in the Middle West, or the Wilsons, marooned in a valley of ashes, the Buchanans have the leisure and wealth to travel wherever they choose. But of course Daisy has not exhausted the world's possibilities, and her declaration suggests that her involvement with life is very superficial. At the same time it conveys a desperate recognition that her life lacks purpose.

A05 KEY INTERPRETATION

A Marxist reading might identify Daisy's lack of purpose as an inevitable consequence of America's class structure and capitalist economic system. While workers in the valley of ashes are 'ash-grey men' who 'move dimly' or 'swarm' to perform their dehumanising work (p. 26), Daisy, despite the superficial glamour and freedom of the privileged class to which she belongs, has lost touch with the world through which she moves, and with her own nature as a human being.

Tom Buchanan

Who is Tom?

- A man who has inherited wealth and is descended from the Scottish gentry.
- He is married to Daisy, but also has an affair with Myrtle Wilson.
- Nick knew him at Yale University, where Tom excelled at American football.

A cruel body

Tom Buchanan is 'a sturdy straw-haired man of thirty, with a rather hard mouth and a supercilious manner' (p. 12). He walks in an 'alert, aggressive way' (p. 169). His eyes are described as shining, arrogant and restless and his body is muscular and very powerful. Nick sums it up as 'a cruel body' (p. 12). Tom comes from an 'enormously wealthy' Midwestern family (p. 11). He likes to display his wealth, and, when he moved to East Egg, he brought a team of polo ponies with him. Tom acknowledges that he is not a popular man.

A simple mind

Nick knew Tom at Yale University, where Tom excelled at American football, rather than in the classroom. Nick now says that Tom has 'a simple mind' (p. 119). In contrast to Gatsby, who has 'an extraordinary gift for hope' (p. 8), Tom is pessimistic about the future. He fears that civilisation is on the verge of collapse, and he holds racist views. Tom refers to books in which he has read the latest scientific theories, but when he refers to them it is clear that he is simply drawn to ideas that seem to support his pessimistic outlook, and that his understanding of science is very limited (see pp. 18, 112 and 116).

KEY CONTEXT — A03

Tom plays polo, a rich person's sport, sometimes known as 'the Sport of Kings'. It is played by two teams of four on horseback. The aim is to drive a small, hard ball into the opposition's goal, using a long wooden mallet. Polo was first played in America in 1876.

KEY QUOTATION — A02

On page 11, Nick notes that when he was a student at Yale University, Tom was 'a national figure in a way, one of those men who reach such an acute limited excellence at twenty-one that everything afterward savours of anti-climax'.

Tom's size and strength equipped him well for the physical demands of American football. But in later life those attributes lend themselves to bullying behaviour. College football gave Tom an outlet for his energies, as well as a degree of celebrity, but it seems that his life peaked too early, and he has failed to develop, intellectually and emotionally.

Progress booster: Racist views — A02

Tom makes several racist comments, including the dramatic declaration: 'It's up to us, who are the dominant race, to watch out or these other races will have control of things' (p. 18). Is racism a character flaw specific to Tom in this novel, or does Fitzgerald present a broader picture of racist attitudes in America?

Adultery

Since the early days of his marriage to Daisy, Tom has had affairs with other women. Throughout the novel he commits adultery with Myrtle Wilson, a working-class woman married to a garage mechanic. Tom uses Myrtle in a cynical way, buying her presents but telling her lies, and when she drunkenly repeats Daisy's name he breaks her nose.

Despite his long-term involvement with mistresses, Tom becomes very moralistic when he feels threatened by Gatsby's love for Daisy. His outburst is hypocritical and characteristically racist: 'Nowadays people begin by sneering at family life and family institutions, and next they'll throw everything overboard and have marriage between black and white' (p. 124).

Jordan Baker

Who is Jordan Baker?

- A golfing celebrity, said to have cheated in a major tournament.
- Daisy's bridesmaid.
- A close friend of Nick.

A modern woman

Jordan Baker is a couple of years younger than Daisy. They grew up together in Louisville, Kentucky, and when Daisy married Tom Buchanan, Jordan acted as her bridesmaid. On the East coast, Jordan lives with her aunt.

Jordan is a slender, sun-tanned young woman with grey eyes and an upright posture. Her hair is said to be 'the colour of an autumn leaf' (p. 168). Nick sums her up as 'this clean, hard, limited person, who dealt in universal scepticism' (p. 77). He tells us that she has a 'bored haughty face' (p. 58) and a 'scornful mouth' (p. 78). Such description presents Jordan in a negative light, especially as she is only in her early twenties, but Nick is attracted to her nonetheless and there are clear indications that they have become more intimately involved than he openly lets on.

Study focus: This hard, clean, limited person **A01**

Why should Jordan, who is clearly attractive, young and talented, be so cynical, bored and scornful? Nick tells us a certain amount about her, but there seems to be much more to her story. Why is she living with her aunt? What actually happened in the golf tournament where she was accused of cheating? Nick fills in details of Gatsby's background, but think carefully about how much he lets us know about the other characters in this novel. Are we led to suspect that Nick knows more about Jordan than he shares with us?

Sport and fair play

When Nick witnesses Jordan telling a lie, he recalls a rumour that she has cheated in a golf tournament. Note how Nick, who prides himself on his ability to reserve judgement, makes the shocking declaration, 'She was incurably dishonest' (p. 58). Is Nick being fair to Jordan here?

Key quotation: Jordan Baker **A02**

On page 168 Jordan says to Nick: 'I thought you were rather an honest, straightforward person. I thought it was your secret pride.'

There are several hints in this novel that the relationship between Nick and Jordan is closer and more complicated than he is prepared to admit. Jordan is generally characterised as coolly resilient and even cynical, but in this conversation she shows herself to be emotionally vulnerable, to value honesty and to have formed a genuine attachment to Nick. The issue of Nick's straightforwardness is of course of vital importance to us, as readers of his narrative.

A03 KEY CONTEXT

The 1920s was a decade when young women, often referred to as 'flappers', exercised unprecedented freedom. They had their hair cut short, wore relatively short skirts and used cosmetics to make themselves more attractive. Fitzgerald, in his short stories, introduced this newly liberated woman into American literature. Jordan is not a 'flapper', simply out to have a wild time, but she is a thoroughly modern young woman, independent and aware of the ways of the world.

George and Myrtle Wilson

Who are the Wilsons?

- George Wilson is a mechanic, who runs a garage; Myrtle is his wife.
- Myrtle is Tom Buchanan's mistress.
- George kills Gatsby after his car, actually driven by Daisy, has killed Myrtle.

Valley of ashes

George Wilson runs a garage in the bleak, dust-covered 'valley of ashes' (p. 26), a spot half-way between West Egg and New York where the city's waste is dumped. George is described as 'a blond, spiritless man, anaemic and faintly handsome' (pp. 26–7). His neighbour, Michaelis, also recognises that spiritless quality, and sees him as 'one of these worn-out men'. He adds that George is 'his wife's man and not his own' (p. 130). Tom Buchanan's dismissive judgement is that George is 'so dumb he doesn't know he's alive' (p. 29). After Myrtle's death George kills Gatsby before taking his own life.

A rich man's world

Myrtle Wilson is Tom Buchanan's mistress. She is in her mid thirties, a few years older than Tom, full-figured and sensual, unlike Daisy who seems to be physically delicate. Seeing Myrtle, Nick remarks that 'there was an immediately perceptible vitality about her as if the nerves of her body were continually smouldering' (p. 28).

Since her marriage, twelve years earlier, Myrtle has helped run the garage. With Tom she is given a glimpse of another world, a world of wealth and leisure. At the apartment, Myrtle puts on ridiculous airs and graces and her laughter is described as 'artificial' (p. 38). She tries to live out the role of a rich man's wife, but then she has to return to her husband and their dismal home above the garage. Tom is determined to keep it that way.

Myrtle met Tom on a train and was dazzled by the clothes he wore. This may remind us of Daisy's response to Gatsby's 'beautiful shirts' (see p. 89). Myrtle was dismayed to find out that George borrowed the suit he wore at their wedding. She says she married him because she thought he was a gentleman, but discovered 'he wasn't fit to lick my shoe' (p. 36). However, her involvement with Tom is her first extra-marital affair. Was she still in love with George when this new world opened up for her? The reality of this new world is made clear when Tom breaks Myrtle's nose merely because she drunkenly repeats Daisy's name.

Progress booster: Parents and children

Myrtle Wilson has a photograph of her mother on the wall of the apartment that Tom keeps for their extra-marital affair. Clearly devoted to her mother's memory, she also plans to buy a wreath for her grave. What light does such devotion shed on other relationships between parents and children in *The Great Gatsby*?

KEY QUOTATION **A02**

On page 152 we read: '"God sees everything," repeated Wilson.'

In his grief and bewilderment Wilson mistakes the eyes on an optician's advertising hoarding for the all-seeing eyes of God. Does Nick see everything in the world he re-creates in his **narrative**? We need to recognise his blind spots.

Meyer Wolfshiem

Who is Meyer Wolfshiem?

- The man who fixed the baseball World Series in 1919.
- One of Gatsby's close associates from the criminal underworld.
- A man who is both sentimental and ruthless.

The criminal underworld

Nick Carraway meets Meyer Wolfshiem at lunch with Gatsby, in Chapter 4. Wolfshiem, fifty years old, is described as 'a small, flat-nosed Jew' with a 'large head' and 'tiny eyes' (p. 68). He recalls people he has known, now 'dead and gone' (p. 68), presumably killed by gangsters. He looks around him apprehensively, inspecting the people in the restaurant, clearly nervous that he might be in danger from some enemy in the world of organised crime.

Wolfshiem wears cuff buttons made from human teeth. This suggests a sinister, even cruel side to Wolfshiem's character, yet his eyes regularly fill with tears. Gatsby says of Wolfshiem, 'He becomes very sentimental sometimes' (p. 71). At such moments he appears soft hearted, but beneath the surface he is a ruthless criminal. Wolfshiem sums up Gatsby's qualities by saying 'There's the kind of man you'd like to take home and introduce to your mother and sister' (p. 70). But remember that Wolfshiem introduces Gatsby not to his mother and sister but to connections in the criminal underworld.

Study focus: Ethnic origins **A01**

Pay close attention to issues of race in *The Great Gatsby*. In a land of equal opportunity, it is clear that certain racial groups are disadvantaged and that family background and ethnic origins play an important role. Wolfshiem has become wealthy, but crime has been his route.

Gatsby's second mentor?

Tom Buchanan alleges that Wolfshiem and Gatsby bought up a lot of general stores and used them to sell alcohol illegally. Nick wonders whether Gatsby too was involved in fixing the 1919 baseball World Series, that major betrayal of the trust of American sports fans. After Gatsby's death, Wolfshiem tells Nick that he actually 'made' Gatsby the man he was: 'I raised him up out of nothing, right out of the gutter' (p. 162). We know that Gatsby inherited no money from Dan Cody, so it is possible that Wolfshiem is telling the truth about the key role he played in his acquisition of wealth.

When Daisy starts to visit Gatsby's house, he dismisses his servants, to prevent gossip. In their place he hires people supplied by Wolfshiem; these associates of a gangster have been trained to keep quiet. Gatsby's chauffeur, 'one of Wolfshiem's protégés' (p. 154), hears the shots fired by George Wilson but doesn't take much notice of them. The implication is that gunshots are not unfamiliar to a man used to living in Wolfshiem's social circle.

A04 **KEY CONNECTION**

Arnold Rothstein, the real-life gangster on whom Meyer Wolfshiem is modelled, was also the inspiration for Nathan Detroit, a character in Damon Runyon's 1933 short story 'The Idyll of Miss Sarah Brown'. That story was the basis for the famous musical *Guys and Dolls*.

A02 **KEY QUOTATION**

On page 71, Gatsby says of Wolfshiem: 'He becomes very sentimental sometimes'. Significantly, this ruthless gambler's tendency towards sentimentality is linked to the passage of time and his awareness of growing older. It colours his recollection of gangster violence at the Metropole, 'Filled with friends gone now forever' (p. 68). Before parting from Gatsby and Nick, Wolfshiem explains that he is fifty years old whereas they belong to a more youthful generation, with different interests. Yet as his narrative unfolds Nick, twenty years younger than Wolfshiem, laments the fact that he too is growing older. Is there evidence to suggest that Nick also 'becomes very sentimental sometimes'?

THEMES

American ideals

Under the red, white, and blue

For a while, Fitzgerald planned to call this book *Under the Red, White, and Blue*. That title invokes the 'Stars and Stripes', the national flag, as an emblem of American ideals.

The American literary critic Lionel Trilling (1905–75) argued that, in a sense, Gatsby *is* America. His character embodies key aspects of the nation's dreams and realities.

As well as telling the story of a glamorous individual, Fitzgerald is addressing the fate of American ideals during a period when the hopes and aspirations expressed in the Declaration of Independence, back in 1776, were being put under pressure or distorted by the materialism, consumerism and violent rivalry of early twentieth-century life.

John Dos Passos (1896–1970), one of the major novelists amongst Fitzgerald's contemporaries, was also disturbed by what he saw as twentieth-century America's abandonment of its fundamental values and founding ideals. His brilliant novel *Manhattan Transfer* (1925) depicts a society where a vast gap has opened between rich and poor and where mean self-interest governs people's actions.

Equality of opportunity

Thomas Jefferson and the other so-called Founding Fathers drafted the Declaration of Independence in 1776, when America broke away from British rule, as a statement of ideals based on equality of opportunity for all. One hundred and fifty years later, Fitzgerald depicts a society divided along lines of social class. The Buchanans and other residents of East Egg live in houses that resemble palaces. The Wilsons, working people, live above their garage in the bleak 'valley of ashes' (p. 26).

KEY CONNECTION   **A03**

With the tough working lives of the Wilsons, compare the plight of the Joads, a poor farming family struggling to survive prolonged drought in the so-called Dust Bowl area of Oklahoma, in John Steinbeck's *The Grapes of Wrath* (1939). Note that the Joads, during the devastating economic depression of the 1930s, go West in search of a better future.

Study focus: Wealth   **A01**

Inherited wealth can result in some living luxuriously without effort, while poor people struggle to survive. *The Great Gatsby* shows how such inequality leads some individuals (Wolfshiem, and Gatsby himself) to engage in crime. But in certain circumstances wealth might be an appropriate reward, or an effective inducement to strive for socially acceptable success. Think carefully and critically about how this novel represents the positive or negative aspects of wealth and ownership in a democratic society.

A peace-loving nation

Jefferson envisaged America as an agrarian society, based on farming and living from the land. But the census of 1920 showed that America had become a predominantly urban nation for the first time. Most Americans now lived in cities, although in reality some of these so-called cities were actually fairly small towns. Note that Jay Gatsby rejects the farming lifestyle of his parents, and after living on Dan Cody's yacht he heads for the city.

Thomas Jefferson also envisaged America as a peace-loving nation. He saw that European societies had been badly damaged by wars, and hoped that America could avoid the waste of human lives in such conflicts. But Fitzgerald stresses the significance to his characters of the First World War (1914–18). In April 1917, America was drawn into this essentially European conflict. Both Nick and Gatsby served in France, in the American army. Gatsby was promoted to the rank of major, which enhanced his social status once the war was over.

America had already experienced the turmoil of Civil War, between 1861 and 1865. The soldiers of the Union (also known as the North) fought against soldiers of the Confederacy (the South) over issues including the continued use of slaves by plantation owners in the South. The North eventually won and slavery in America came to an end. But over 600,000 soldiers died, and the American ideal of living peacefully was shattered.

Individualism

America has traditionally cherished the notion of individuals being able to live with minimal interference or regulation from the government. In the view of Thomas Jefferson, 'That government is best which governs least.'

The Great Gatsby portrays an American society in which individuals have recently been drafted into the army to go to war, and then subjected to Prohibition laws during peacetime. We are told that, as a young officer, Jay Gatsby 'was liable at the whim of an impersonal government to be blown anywhere about the world' (p. 142). The novel also reflects the emergence of a mass society in which the individual may be influenced, often without knowing it, by the persuasive power of advertising and fashion, cinema, radio and magazines. Individuality becomes a complex issue in such a society.

Revision task 8: Gatsby and America A02

Make notes summarising what you understand by the following assertions:

- Jay Gatsby *is* America.
- *The Great Gatsby* portrays the reality of American society as a betrayal of American ideals.

Key quotation: American ideals A02

On page 160, Henry Gatz says of his son: 'If he'd of lived, he'd of been a great man.'

The novel's title *The Great Gatsby* is difficult to justify from the knowledge we have of Jay Gatsby's life. It is not easy to find greatness in his criminality or his obsessive pursuit of Daisy. Perhaps it is here, in his father's vision of a future that will never materialise, that the real 'Great Gatsby' can be found. Note that Gatz envisages him helping to 'build up the country' (p. 1   ) like the Minnesota railway pioneer James J. Hill. Greatness is, in this imagined fut   related to collective benefit and social good rather than a dream of personal fulfi

---

A03 PROGRESS BOOSTER

The Great Gatsby raises many questions about identity. For example, are you really in control of your own identity if you are what you wear, or if you are defined by the car you drive or the house in which you live? Does Fitzgerald suggest that young James Gatz, roaming the shore of Lake Superior, had more integrity as an individual than Jay Gatsby, living with an image borrowed from the European upper class, wearing imported clothes, driving a British car and using the affected phrase 'old sport'? Think carefully about how individualism and identity are connected in this novel.

A03 KEY CONTEXT

In 1922, the year in which the action of *The Great Gatsby* is set, Herbert Hoover, president of the United States, published a book called *American Individualism*, in which he reflected on the First World War and the recent revolution in Russia. Hoover asserted his faith in a 'progressive individualism' that was specifically American, and which encouraged development of manual skills, intellect and spirituality, as well as offering equality of opportunity. The schedule drawn up by James Gatz in 1906 (p. 164) is a blueprint for such personal development. But Fitzgerald's tragic tale casts such aspirations in an **ironic** light.

The American Dream

A matter of infinite hope

The American Dream is a very familiar phrase, but what does it actually mean? In its most positive sense, the American Dream means that in this land of opportunities, anything is possible and anyone can be a success, no matter what their background. When Nick Carraway refers to Gatsby's 'extraordinary gift for hope' (p. 8), we are being encouraged to recognise Gatsby as an embodiment of the American Dream.

Self-improvement

A closely related version of the American Dream has a more practical side; it suggests that if you work hard and live an honest and respectable life, you are bound to improve your position in the world. This is the American Dream that is reflected in the schedule drawn up by young James Gatz in his copy of the book *Hopalong Cassidy*. Here, he resolves to rise from bed at 6 a.m., and then at specifically allocated times to study, to work and to improve his way of speaking and his physical posture. He also resolves 'Be better to parents' (p. 164).

Get rich quick

The American Dream has also come to mean simply getting rich quickly. It's that materialistic version of the Dream that Gatsby seems to fulfil when he makes enough money in just three years to buy his huge mansion in West Egg village. We are led to believe that it was not hard work that enabled him to make this lavish purchase, but criminal activity.

Across the bay, in East Egg, there are houses like palaces that belong to people such as the Buchanans, who have inherited wealth and have not needed to work for material success. George Wilson, on the other hand, who labours daily at his garage, remains poor and lives in the bleak 'valley of ashes' (p. 26). This vast gap between the privileged and the disadvantaged seems a betrayal of the American ideal of equal opportunity for all.

 A03

Progress booster: New beginnings

An important aspect of the American Dream has been the possibility of making a fresh start. Gatsby tries to re-create himself, concealing the past and apparently abandoning his parents. This might suggest a parallel with the way America tried to cast off the past, to break away from European history and Old World values, when the new nation issued its Declaration of Independence in 1776. Does *The Great Gatsby* suggest that new beginnings are really possible? Or does it show that the present and future are shaped by the past?

Key quotation: The American Dream **A03**

On page 159 Henry Gatz says of his son: 'He had a big future before him'; and on page 164, he repeats the point: 'he had a big future in front of him'.

Note that, although Gatz is proud of his son's achievement (as he understands it), it is Gatsby's unfulfilled potential that he stresses. In its purest form, the American Dream characteristically looks to the future; it is less about attaining a specific goal than about moving into new realms of possibility. Making Daisy the focus for his 'big future' was arguably Gatsby's tragic error, as it dragged him back into the long-lost past and narrowed his horizons in a way that betrayed his 'extraordinary gift for hope' (p. 8).

KEY CONTEXT **A04**

Hopalong Cassidy (1910) was a widely read tale of the West, written by Clarence E. Mulford (1883–1956). Numerous sequels were published featuring the cowboy hero, who gave his name to the book's title. Starting in 1934, a series of Hopalong Cassidy films were made. Later there was also a television series. Ask yourself why such tales of the American West have proved to be enduringly popular.

KEY CONTEXT **A03**

The schedule found inside James Gatz's copy of *Hopalong Cassidy* is based on a famous plan for efficient organisation of each day in Benjamin Franklin's posthumously published *Autobiography* (1818). Benjamin Franklin (1706–90), one of America's Founding Fathers, extolled the value of hard work, honesty and discipline as keys to both spiritual and material success. He was a highly educated and sophisticated man, but practical too and well known as an inventor.

The Frontier

Heading West

Near the end of *The Great Gatsby* there is a famous image of Dutch sailors, experiencing a sense of wonder as they encountered for the first time 'a fresh, green breast of the new world' (p. 171). Early settlers from Europe spoke of America as the New World in opposition to the Old World they had left behind.

As the East coast of America became settled, with towns and later cities, Americans continued to move further across the continent, heading West. Despite the presence of Native Americans, who were there long before the Europeans, the West was regarded by these later arrivals as an empty space where it was possible to make a fresh start. The boundary between the settled land and the empty space was known as the Frontier.

In 1893, a history professor named Frederick Jackson Turner (1861–1932) published an essay entitled 'The Significance of the Frontier in American History'. Turner claimed that the Frontier had produced a distinctive American spirit, democratic in a very practical way and relatively free from European influence. The West, he suggested, held the promise of freedom for everyone. It offered the means to live and provided possibilities for personal development.

By the time Turner was writing, settlement had already extended across America and there was no longer a real Frontier. The Frontier, with its distinctive spirit, has remained a powerful idea in American culture, however. American space travel, leaving Earth behind, may be seen as a way of opening up another Frontier, and pushing back the boundaries.

The Midwest in *The Great Gatsby*

'I see now that this has been a story of the West, after all', declares Nick Carraway in Chapter 9 (p. 167). On a literal level, he seems to mean that all the main characters are from the Midwest, the geographical heart of America. None are actually from the West coast, where America meets the Pacific Ocean, although at one point Gatsby claims, untruthfully, to be from San Francisco (see p. 64). Nick has gone East to work in finance, but has returned home to the Midwest to write his book.

The Midwest is presented as a place where you still find basic American values, such as honesty, trust and even innocence. From his brief appearance in the book, Gatsby's father, Henry C. Gatz, seems to have these qualities, yet in Gatsby's eyes his father is a failure.

Nick prides himself on being honest, but at the end of the book Jordan says she was mistaken when she took Nick to be 'rather an honest, straightforward person' (p. 168). Jordan herself is cynical and a cheat; Daisy at times seems weak and shallow; Tom is violent and bigoted. In what way is this 'a story of the West, after all' we may wonder?

A03 **KEY CONTEXT**

Henry Nash Smith's *Virgin Land: The American West as Symbol and Myth* (Harvard University Press, 1974) is a fascinating study of the role the West has played in the way America sees itself. It contains sections on Thomas Jefferson and his ideals, the frontiersman as Western hero, the myth of the New World garden, and the classic analysis of the Frontier offered by American historian Frederick Jackson Turner.

Key quotation: The Frontier   **A02**

On page 167, Nick declares: 'I see now that this has been a story of the West, after all.'

It is 'a story of the West', above all perhaps because it locates value in innocence and dreams rather than in cynicism and despair. But Nick has a tendency to make statements of this kind, not definitive in their meaning but rich in potential significance. That is part of the reason why this novel is so thought-provoking, even after you have read it several times. It may also be part of the crucially American nature of *The Great Gatsby*: a text about possible meanings rather than a fixed interpretation.

Desire and wonder

Study focus: 'Unutterable visions'   A02

Gatsby's greatness, for Nick, seems to reside in his capacity for hope and the persistence of his desire. Daisy is the immediate object of that desire, but Nick says Gatsby's hunger for the possibilities that life has to offer 'had gone beyond her, beyond everything' (p. 92).

Nick tells us that to kiss Daisy will not fulfil Gatsby: 'He knew that when he kissed this girl, and forever wed his unutterable visions to her perishable breath, his mind would never romp again like the mind of God' (p. 107). Those 'unutterable visions' are what really motivate Gatsby. It is not so much a specific goal, but Gatsby's intense desire to change the conditions of his own life, his striving to change, that makes him great in Nick's eyes.

Lack of purpose

Fitzgerald contrasts the intensity of Gatsby's desire with the cynicism and purposelessness of those around him. Daisy, still in her early twenties, complains that she has 'been everywhere and seen everything and done everything' (p. 22). She cannot imagine that the future holds anything new for her, and the prospect of having to devise ways to spend the years ahead simply appals her. The people she knows also suffer from this lack of purpose. They drift, restless but without direction.

A sense of wonder

At the end of the novel, Nick writes: 'I thought of Gatsby's wonder when he first picked out the green light at the end of Daisy's dock' (p. 171). Coming immediately after Nick's reference to Dutch sailors arriving at America's East coast, finding themselves 'face to face for the last time in history with something commensurate to his capacity for wonder' (p. 171), Gatsby's sense of wonder might seem trivial. It might indicate the limitations of Gatsby's imagination that he finds a green electric light so awesome. Compared to Daisy's jaded outlook, however, Gatsby's sense of wonder can be seen to bring the world alive for him. His world can still appear enchanted and radiant.

Revision task 9: Gatsby's desire   A02

Make notes to show how you would support or argue against the claim that Gatsby desires Daisy because of what she represents rather than who she is. Refer to their first meeting in Louisville, but also to later encounters in New York.

Key quotation: Desire and wonder   A02

On page 107 Nick writes of 'the incomparable milk of wonder'.

The quality of wonder suggests childlike innocence, entirely free from world-weariness. The figurative use of 'milk' links wonder to the feeding of an infant, as though an individual's healthy growth requires such nourishment and stimulation of the imagination as the experience of wonder can provide. This image of a nurturing breast is in stark contrast to the mutilation Myrtle suffers when hit by a car. Note though the recurrence of the word wonder on p. 171, where the Dutch sailor looking at the land that will be America is said to be 'face to face for the last time in history with something commensurate to his capacity for wonder'.

Vision and insight

A maker of spectacles

Gatsby is a maker of spectacles in the sense that he throws parties that are intended to be seen by Daisy across the bay. The clothes he wears, the cars he drives, the extravagance of his house are all part of the display – all part of the spectacle.

Doctor T. J. Eckleburg is a maker of spectacles in another sense; he makes eye-glasses that correct physical distortions in vision. One of the most striking images in *The Great Gatsby* presents the eyes of T. J. Eckleburg, looming over the 'valley of ashes' (p. 26). This advertising hoarding is a **realistic** detail from the landscape of 1920s America, but it is also a focal point for the novel's theme of vision, its limits and potential.

At a crucial point in the **narrative**, Michaelis finds his neighbour, George Wilson, staring at the optician's hoarding. Wilson, in a deeply disturbed state following the death of his wife, says, 'God sees everything'. Michaelis tries to correct him, pointing out 'That's an advertisement' (p. 152). But George now sees everything differently. Seeing clearly is not always a straightforward business in this novel.

Point of view

Nick Carraway is narrating Gatsby's story as he saw it, but he knows there are other versions which might be told from other points of view. Fitzgerald portrays 1920s America as a world where speculation and gossip spread rapidly, based on partial knowledge. Nick concedes early on that 'life is much more successfully looked at from a single window, after all' (p. 10). Should we agree with that statement? Gatsby, obsessive in his desire for Daisy, seems to look at life 'from a single window', but ultimately that doesn't appear to be a successful way of seeing life. At the end of Chapter 7, Nick leaves Gatsby standing in the moonlight, 'watching over nothing' (p. 139).

A visionary?

Images of sight and seeing occur often in *The Great Gatsby*. Genuine insight is more rare however. Owl Eyes, the visitor to Gatsby's party who wears owl-eyed spectacles, may have the appearance of wisdom conventionally associated with owls, his spectacles may make him look scholarly, but he has in fact been drunk for a week. He is impressed by the realistic effect Gatsby has created in his library, rather than by anything worthwhile that may be learnt there. Owl Eyes appreciates the lengths Gatsby has gone to in projecting his image through spectacles, but he shows no interest in what lies beyond the surface.

Is Jay Gatsby simply a showman? Or are we invited to see him as a visionary, someone who can see beyond what is to what might be? Gatsby fixes his gaze on the green light at the end of Daisy's dock, but through that he sees a host of 'unutterable visions' (p. 107). Is Gatsby a man who deludes himself and tries to hoodwink the world by creating illusions? Or is the capacity to imagine the world differently a true measure of greatness?

A05 KEY INTERPRETATION

A Feminist critical approach might focus upon the way Gatsby's fixation with Daisy reduces her from a flesh-and-blood human being to the passive object of his gaze. In such a reading, Gatsby's devotion to the girl of his dreams, concentrated into his act of staring across the bay, is recognised as a form of patriarchal oppression. In response to such an argument, you might ask whether Gatsby is really looking at Daisy or whether he is actually watching himself, infatuated not with her but with his own image as a lover and a dreamer.

Codes of conduct

Firm foundations

At the start of his narration, Nick says that after the turbulence of the war he wanted the world 'to be in uniform and at a sort of moral attention forever' (p. 8). He means that he wanted the world to become a disciplined and orderly place, where you knew what was what. Instead, he finds himself in a world filled with uncertainty and unpredictability.

In Chapter 6, Nick writes about Gatsby's teenage dreams and remarks that Gatsby's 'heart was in a constant turbulent riot' (p. 95). This seems to be just the kind of turmoil that Nick now wants to avoid; he goes on to say that these dreams offered Gatsby 'a promise that the rock of the world was founded securely on a fairy's wing' (p. 96). Gatsby has abandoned the schedule he had earlier drawn up as a guideline for his life. Instead, he is now guided by his imagination.

Would Nick consider that a sufficiently firm foundation for a code of conduct? Might the 'fairy's wing', the power of imagination, be just as good a foundation for a code of conduct as 'the hard rock' of military discipline?

Fitzgerald develops this theme in various ways. Is it better to live a cautious and disciplined existence, as Nick says he does, or to live passionately, like Gatsby? The former way of life offers security; the latter has intensity, but is dangerous. Nick's **ambivalence** towards Gatsby is really focused on this question of how best to live one's life. At the start he says that Gatsby 'represented everything for which I have an unaffected scorn' (p. 8). Yet he admires Gatsby's capacity to dream, to desire and to hope, and out of respect for that he has written this account of Gatsby's life.

Honesty and fair play

In *The Great Gatsby* it seems to be difficult to be honest, even in sport, which depends upon fair behaviour as well as clear codes of conduct. Jordan Baker cheats at golf, and Meyer Wolfshiem fixes the outcome of the baseball World Series. And what of Gatsby's favourite phrase, 'old sport'? It seems to invoke fair play, but in fact it is just an empty affectation.

Nick takes pride in his own honesty. It would be comforting to believe that we are reading an account written by a man we can trust. But can we really trust Nick? Is he being honest about his reasons for admiring Jay Gatsby? Does he honestly believe what he tells us about himself? Remember that near the end Jordan says to him that she believed he was honest, but now realises that she has been mistaken: 'I thought you were rather an honest, straightforward person. I thought it was your secret pride' (p. 168).

Key quotation: Codes of conduct **A02**

On pages 7–8, Nick declares: 'Conduct may be founded on the hard rock or the wet marshes, but after a certain point I don't care what it's founded on.'

In the aftermath of the First World War, Nick craves an orderly life. This may be a consequence of the discipline he experienced as a soldier, or it may be that he fears the chaos and disorder which the war in Europe brought with it. As a writer and **narrator**, he may recognise that a reliable code of conduct allows accurate interpretation of people's behaviour. But can we be sure that Nick himself is reliable and that his interpretations are accurate? He says after a certain point he doesn't care what the foundations for such a code of conduct might be, but we might question the wisdom of ignoring the grounds upon which rules of behaviour are based.

KEY CONNECTION **A04**

With Nick's desire for a code of conduct, compare the inability of Frederic Henry, narrator of Ernest Hemingway's *A Farewell to Arms* (1929), to accept the terms on which the First World War is fought. Unable to find a basis for his own conduct in religion, patriotism or conventional morality, Henry initially seeks to lose himself through heavy drinking and sexual encounters. With no external guidance as to how he should behave in the world, Henry is ultimately thrown back upon his own sense of what is right for him, as an individual in any given situation.

PROGRESS CHECK

Section One: Check your understanding

These short tasks will help you to evaluate your knowledge and skills level in this particular area.

1. What evidence is there that Gatsby is a criminal? Make notes listing at least three points.

2. 'A weakness of this novel is that none of the characters is truly likeable.' List four to five points in support of or arguing against this view.

3. What is the significance of Pammy Buchanan's presence in this novel? Write a paragraph explaining your view.

4. Make a table listing four or five key points of difference between the lives led by the Wilsons and by the Buchanans.

5. Identify three statements or events within Nick's **narrative** that shed light on his relationships with women; in each case briefly explain what is revealed about his character.

6. List four events or circumstances in the novel that reveal a failure of American ideals. In each case, briefly describe the nature of that failure.

7. What is the thematic significance of the character known as Owl Eyes? Write a paragraph discussing your ideas.

8. Identify four ways in which desire is made manifest through action or behaviour in this novel.

9. How are the references to sport in the novel related to its thematic concern with codes of conduct? Write a paragraph outlining your ideas.

10. How does Nick's narrative show social class to be a significant issue? List five events and briefly explain the significance of each.

Section Two: Working towards the exam

Choose one of the following three tasks which require longer, more developed answers:

1. 'Jay Gatsby embodies a clash between American ideals and American history.' Do you agree?

2. 'Nick's personal pessimism is responsible for the jaundiced view of the American Dream in this novel.' To what extent do you agree with this viewpoint?

3. Compare the depiction of success and failure in *The Great Gatsby* with the way they are depicted in any other American novel you have studied.

A01 **PROGRESS BOOSTER**

For each Section Two task, read the question carefully, select the key areas you need to address, and plan an essay of six or seven points. Write a first draft, giving yourself an hour to do so. Make sure you include supporting evidence for each point, including quotations.

Progress check (rate your understanding on a level of 1 – low, to 5 – high)	1	2	3	4	5
The key actions, motives and thoughts of major and minor characters in the text					
The different ways you can interpret particular characters' words and actions					
How characterisation is linked to key themes and ideas					
The significance of key themes and ideas within the text					
How some key themes (such as the American West) are linked to context					

GENRE

Tragedy

Tragedy is a literary genre with a long history. Aeschylus, Sophocles and Euripides wrote tragic plays in the fifth century BC. Characteristically these involve the downfall of a noble protagonist who, striving to achieve some goal, is frustrated by intervention of the gods or by adverse circumstances, compounded by the effect of some personal flaw or an error of judgement. Sometimes, this reversal of fortunes results in the death of the hero; often, however, it is accompanied by a clearer understanding of the nature of human life.

Hamlet, Othello, King Lear and *Macbeth* – well-known tragic dramas written by William Shakespeare during the first decade of the seventeenth century – all involve the downfall and death of an exceptional individual.

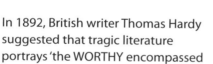

Ask yourself whether tragedy is an appropriate genre for a modern democratic society in which citizens are, in basic respects, equal. Can we regard the fate of an individual living in a mass society as tragic? Can the death of Jay Gatsby in 1922 be seen in a tragic light, given the death of millions during the First World War, just a few years earlier?

In 1892, British writer Thomas Hardy suggested that tragic literature portrays 'the WORTHY encompassed by the INEVITABLE'. In this definition, tragedy occurs when an individual whose virtue or merit is obvious suffers because they have no control over a course of events that unfolds with a kind of mechanical inevitability, indifferent to the fate of an individual. Is Jay Gatsby worthy? Is his death inevitable?

In his 1949 essay 'Tragedy and the Common Man', American dramatist Arthur Miller redefined the tragic hero as an ordinary person struggling to maintain human dignity. Jay Gatsby has raised his social status, but is his rise to wealth a dignified process? Is 'The Great Gatsby' a tragic hero or merely a deluded egotist who lacks dignity and throws his life away?

Frame narratives

In the European Middle Ages, frame **narratives** were used as a neat way to gather collections of disparate stories. Giovanni Boccaccio's *Decameron* (*c*.1350) is framed by an account of ten people who have fled from plague to a villa outside Florence, where they tell one hundred stories. The frame for Geoffrey Chaucer's long narrative poem *The Canterbury Tales* (*c*.1380) tells of a pilgrimage, with each of the travellers narrating a story during the journey.

Modern novelists have recognised that frame narratives offer great potential for increasing the psychological and thematic richness of a story. Fitzgerald was particularly impressed by the depth of meaning achieved by such means in Joseph Conrad's *Heart of Darkness* (1899) and *Lord Jim* (1900). His own frame narrative for *The Great Gatsby* tells of Nick Carraway's return to the Middle West where he settled down to write an account of events that happened in New York. Nick's **point of view** as narrator thus becomes an explicit ingredient in the novel, which we need to take into account as we read it.

KEY CONNECTION

Fitzgerald's subtle narrative technique in *The Great Gatsby* might fruitfully be compared with the multiple points of view created by American modernist William Faulkner (1897–1962) in his novel *The Sound and the Fury* (1929). Faulkner's numerous novels tend to return to the same Southern settings, characters and themes, yet show them in a varying light by means of different narrative styles and techniques.

STRUCTURE

Looking for clues

The fact that Nick Carraway is both the **narrator** of *The Great Gatsby* and a character in the story he tells has implications for the structure of the book. Nick's narration essentially involves telling us what he has found out about Jay Gatsby. He also conveys to us his feelings about this man and the events that lead to his death. In doing so, Nick reveals aspects of his own character.

Nick is rather like a detective, finding clues and interpreting them, trying to track down the real Jay Gatsby. In sharing this experience with us, Nick releases information gradually, bit by bit, so we too can have the experience of coming to know Gatsby. All the action of the story has already happened. In part Nick seems to be using the act of narration to make things clearer in his own mind. There remain aspects of Gatsby about which we are uncertain at the end; there are still elements of mystery. A further complication is that while reading his account we may find that we don't fully trust Nick. We are, after all, finding out about him too.

Study focus: Clues

A01

The structure of *The Great Gatsby* involves a trail of clues, some misleading, some helpful. Our task, which is also one of the book's great pleasures, is not just to follow a story but also to decipher the clues. Patterns of words and images emerge and, as careful readers, we need to recognise them and try to discover their meaning.

Intricate patterning

The composition of *The Great Gatsby* involves intricate patterns in which certain words, images and events **foreshadow** or echo others. For example, colour words – notably green, white and gold – recur regularly, applied to very different objects. Familiar associations of these colours, such as the association of green with Nature, are modified as the words appear in differing contexts. 'White' is applied to the 'palaces' of the wealthy (p. 11), and to the 'ashen dust' that coats George Wilson's clothes (p. 28). Daisy refers to her 'white girlhood' in the American Midwest (p. 24), which might appear to mean one thing in relation to her white dress (p. 13), but quite another in the context of Tom's remarks on the supposed superiority of the white race (p. 18).

The Great Gatsby is not structured in a straightforward way. Nick Carraway wants us to notice the words: his vocabulary is at times obscure and difficult (words such as 'meretricious', 'postern' and 'orgastic'); his imagery can be elaborate and artificial ('now the orchestra is playing yellow cocktail music', p. 42). Nick is being self-consciously literary and is, in effect, reminding us that he is in the process of becoming a writer as this narrative unfolds. The patterning of the novel reflects Nick's activity not only as a kind of detective, on the trail of Jay Gatsby, but also as a writer, creating *The Great Gatsby*. Nick Carraway has a poetic imagination beneath his prosaic surface.

A03 **KEY CONTEXT**

The 1920s and 1930s are regarded as the 'Golden Age of Detective Fiction'. American writers such as Dashiell Hammett (1894–1961) and Raymond Chandler (1888–1959) worked in this genre during the ten years after *The Great Gatsby* was published. Although Fitzgerald's novel is not detective fiction, it contains some ingredients of that genre: a murder, a suicide, a hit-and-run incident, shady figures from the criminal underworld, a character shrouded in mystery and another (Nick Carraway) who reserves judgement while tracking down the facts.

LANGUAGE

The first-person narrator

The most important literary technique utilised by Fitzgerald in *The Great Gatsby* was recognised immediately by his editor, Maxwell Perkins. Perkins told the author in November 1924 that he felt his book used the most appropriate method for telling the story – a **narrator** who is a participant in that story, but is more a spectator than an actor. This creates a complex **point of view**, which involves us, as readers, in acts of interpretation that necessarily extend to making judgements about Nick Carraway.

We experience the immediacy of being addressed by a first-person voice. But we find Nick making carefully formulated and considered comments such as this: 'Instead of rambling, this party had preserved a dignified homogeneity, and assumed to itself the function of representing the staid nobility of the countryside – East Egg condescending to West Egg and carefully on guard against its spectroscopic gaiety' (p. 46).

The narrator has weighed up the situation and lets us share his conclusion in a sentence that is not easy to understand. It is densely written, and uses sophisticated vocabulary. Words such as 'homogeneity', 'staid' and 'spectroscopic' convey that Nick is an educated man; they seem to add weight to a judgement made by a man who is keeping his distance.

Study focus: Presenting Gatsby

The success of this novel depends heavily upon Fitzgerald's control of how the figure of Jay Gatsby is presented to us. He has to be filtered through Nick Carraway's narration at a suitable pace and with appropriate emphasis to sustain our interest without dispelling the necessary element of mystery. Expressing at the outset his reservations about Gatsby as well as his admiration for him, Nick himself becomes a figure we must interpret. Bear in mind that, as we are piecing together the puzzle of Gatsby, we are also modifying our sense of Nick, the man who is telling Gatsby's story.

The narrator as participant

Despite his reserve, Nick becomes thoroughly caught up in events: 'I was enjoying myself now. I had taken two finger-bowls of champagne, and the scene had changed before my eyes into something significant, elemental, and profound' (p. 48).

He is still concerned to give us his sense of events, and he is still self-conscious in his use of language, but we are now being addressed by someone sitting in Gatsby's garden, sipping champagne, being part of the action. The form of the novel combines storytelling with interpretation. That interpretation is continuously adjusted, tweaked as Nick sees the events he is describing in a slightly different light.

A complex protagonist

As it is, Jay Gatsby, filtered little by little through Nick Carraway's narration, presents an intriguingly complex figure, who is able to carry the weight of associations from American history and myth that Fitzgerald chose to place upon him. The novel's form is largely a result of the way in which Nick's narrative is paced, with a gradual release of vital clues and illuminating information.

Dialogue and the scenic method

Varying the voice

The story is narrated from Nick Carraway's **point of view**. Fitzgerald must have been acutely aware that this involved potential dangers. For example, Nick's voice might have come to seem monotonous, his manner of expression too self-conscious, or his interest in events too narrow.

Fitzgerald avoids this pitfall by letting Nick, writing his own account of events, give us dramatic exchanges in **dialogue**. Nick mimics the idiosyncrasies of a range of voices, for example, Gatsby's cool delivery and the affectation of his favourite phrase, 'old sport'; Jordan Baker's pointed observations, cynical but often revealing; or Meyer Wolfshiem's stylised Jewish accent.

If Fitzgerald had focused closely on the workings of Nick Carraway's mind, as he mulled over the significance of what he had witnessed, we would probably now have a slow-paced and rather turgid novel. The kind of self-analysis Nick gives us in the opening paragraphs of the book is fine for a few pages, but if sustained for the entire novel, it would make for heavy reading.

Scenic method

Instead we get a series of dramatic reconstructions. So, in Chapter 2, Nick takes us into the apartment where Tom Buchanan and Myrtle Wilson conduct their extra-marital affair. We hear them talk, and violently squabble as they get drunk. Or in Chapter 4, Nick takes us to a restaurant on New York's Forty-second Street, where we meet Meyer Wolfshiem and discover how close his friendship with Gatsby has actually been.

In *The Great Gatsby*, each of these scenes is self-contained, yet it echoes or **foreshadows** other parts of the narrative and contains elaborate cross-references. The party in Chapter 2, in Tom and Myrtle's apartment, is paralleled by the party at the Plaza Hotel in Chapter 7. Larger parties are held at Gatsby's mansion, in Chapters 3 and 6. In this way, a formal symmetry is constructed. At the centre of the book, in Chapter 5, Nick and Daisy are reunited over tea at Nick's house.

So Nick's narrative combines his own commentary with lively and varied dramatic scenes that feature skilfully crafted dialogue. The dialogue assists the unfolding of the story. It also serves to develop characterisation, giving us insights into the nature and attitudes of the speakers. We, as readers, are invited to listen in to the conversations, to observe the action and to take note of the body language. Then we may draw our own conclusions.

A04 KEY CONNECTION

Fitzgerald admired the use of this scenic method of narrative construction in the work of American novelist Henry James (1843–1916). Henry James had tried to write plays for the theatre. His efforts were unsuccessful, but he learnt from the experience and began to incorporate dramatic scenes, comparable to those found in stage plays, into his fiction. A good example of his scenic method can be found in the novel *The Portrait of a Lady* (1881), which incorporates a series of carefully 'stage-managed' scenes.

Study focus: Reading events **A01**

Nick gives us his interpretation of events and characters, but in these dramatic interludes we feel that we are witnessing some of those events first hand, and are actually meeting those characters. The impact is more direct. Yet that means there is scope for disagreement to arise between Nick's conclusions and our own reading of events, especially when he is assessing his own role in the action. Look carefully at the complex relationship between these dramatic set pieces (actually narrated by Nick, of course) and the commentary he supplies.

Cinematic techniques

Although we might say that *The Great Gatsby* is essentially a novel about a man writing a book, and although Nick Carraway often uses language in a very self-conscious way, this is also a novel that creates strong visual impressions. Cinema was a relatively new art form when Fitzgerald was writing. It is tempting to view his visual effects, such as the lighting of Gatsby's parties or his striking descriptions of clothing and postures, in cinematic terms.

Remember that films were still silent when Fitzgerald wrote this book; 'talkies' came in a couple of years later. Films were almost exclusively made in black and white, as modern colour techniques were not then available. Editing techniques were far less sophisticated than they are now. But the use of the scenic method, and transitions between one scene and another, gives parts of *The Great Gatsby* a cinematic feel.

Fitzgerald's final novel, *The Last Tycoon* (1941), left unfinished at his death, is set in Hollywood, California. He lived there from 1937, working as a scriptwriter, and died there in 1940. The advent of 'talkies' at the end of the 1920s attracted some serious writers, including John Steinbeck (1902–68) and William Faulkner (1897–1962), to Hollywood, where their skill in scripting dialogue was in great demand and they could make money.

In *The Great Gatsby*, Fitzgerald employs some techniques which might be indebted to the example of the cinema. The most evident is the cut, which he uses to make sudden transitions from one scene to another. Chapter 4 furnishes good examples with the cut from Gatsby's car to a cellar restaurant where he has lunch with Wolfshiem (p. 67), and the cut from that cellar restaurant to the Plaza Hotel where Nick is taking tea with Jordan (p. 72). Chapter 7, in which Myrtle Wilson is killed, relies heavily upon such clean cuts from one scene to another.

In those scenes where small parties occur (at Tom and Myrtle's apartment in Chapter 2 and at the Plaza Hotel in Chapter 7) and in those scenes where large parties are given by Gatsby, we find techniques that can be read in terms of cinematic practice. There are movements, for example, from close-ups to panoramic shots, from focus on an individual character to an overview of the crowd and the setting. Such readings are particularly tempting as Gatsby's house and garden are artificially lit like a film set. Note the care with which Fitzgerald handles lighting effects throughout the novel.

Nick refers to 'the great burst of leaves growing on the trees, just as things grow in fast movies' (p. 9). This comparison between rapidly growing foliage and the action in a speeded-up film shows how attuned Fitzgerald had already become to the new cinematic medium, and the kinds of altered perception it allowed.

KEY CONTEXT **A04**

The most recent film adaptation of *The Great Gatsby* was released in 2012. The first – silent and in black and white – appeared in November 1926, based upon a play, adapted from Fitzgerald's novel by American dramatist Owen Davis (1874–1956). Does *The Great Gatsby* lend itself to cinematic treatment? What might be lost, or gained, in a film version? You might also think about how other novels have fared in big-screen adaptations (for example: *The Adventures of Huckleberry Finn*, *Sister Carrie*, *A Farewell to Arms* or *The Grapes of Wrath*).

The written word

Reading some novels, you are scarcely aware of the words on the page. Instead, it feels as if you are watching the characters and the action directly. But in *The Great Gatsby* we are often made aware of the words. Nick is not always inviting us to look through a transparent window and see what Gatsby is up to; he is writing his own account of Gatsby, and the writing is often what we see.

Sentences such as 'In his blue gardens men and girls came and went like moths among the whisperings and the champagne and the stars' (p. 41), or 'The moon had risen higher, and floating in the Sound was a triangle of silver scales, trembling a little to the stiff, tinny drip of the banjoes on the lawn' (p. 48), make a vivid appeal to the senses, yet we are still aware of Nick self-consciously at work, trying to introduce poetic concentration into his prose – and succeeding.

Vocabulary

Nick, educated at Yale University, doesn't shy away from words that might be unfamiliar to many readers. His vocabulary can seem difficult. For example, he suggests that Gatsby has lived in the service of 'a vast, vulgar, and meretricious beauty' (p. 95). The uncommon word 'meretricious' means flashy, or attractive in a shallow way, and it derives from a Latin word for prostitute. Once we understand this, it sheds some light on Gatsby; but before we understand its actual meaning 'meretricious' has already told us that Nick is well educated and has literary aspirations – he is choosing his words carefully as he writes.

Words in action

Language communicates meaning, but it can also create special effects within our understanding. Words can do things on the page that make us think differently or in a more complex way. Wolfshiem is said to eat with 'ferocious delicacy' (p. 69). An adjective is coupled with a noun that seems to contradict it, creating an **oxymoron**. This seems to fit with Wolfshiem's character, which is both sentimental and ruthless.

Fitzgerald knew that words, written or spoken, can perform functions that are not simply about carrying meaning. During the encounter between Tom and Gatsby in Chapter 7, we are told that 'The words seemed to bite physically into Gatsby' (p. 126). Tom uses language not just to convey a message, but also to bully. On the next page we find, 'Tom's words suddenly leaned down over Gatsby' (p. 127).

Revision task 10: A man writing a book **A02**

Make notes to clarify your understanding of the contention that *The Great Gatsby* is essentially a novel about a man writing a book. You should think about Nick's motivation for telling us this story, taking into account his literary leanings at Yale, his taste for poetic imagery and unfamiliar vocabulary, and the lack of personal fulfilment offered by his work as a bondsman.

A02 KEY INTERPRETATION

The phrase 'ferocious delicacy' (p. 69) may bring to mind Daisy, 'winking ferociously' (p. 18). Later, we encounter the phrase 'ferocious indifference' (p. 96). Use of the adjective 'ferocious' and adverb 'ferociously', with nouns and a verb that they do not really fit, hints at intense feelings lurking beneath the surface of daily life. At times in this novel that intensity finds an outlet, in the form of wild pleasure-seeking or physical violence. Remember that just a few years earlier the First World War had exposed an unimaginable ferocity lurking beneath the polite surface of supposedly civilised societies.

Symbolism

In literature a symbol is an image, an object or action used to represent an idea or a set of associations. We encounter symbolism in daily life too. Take the familiar example of status symbols. These feature extensively in the social world of *The Great Gatsby*, where an expensive shirt, an imported car or a large house may represent wealth, class or a sophisticated lifestyle.

Symbolism is an important literary device for Fitzgerald because it allows him to show how the meaning of a word can expand or contract according to the context in which it is used. The closing reference to 'a fresh green breast of the new world' (p. 171) uses the image of a nurturing breast in relation to the discovery by Europeans of the American continent. An earlier image of a breast depicts young Gatsby sucking, **metaphorically**, 'the incomparable milk of wonder' from 'the pap of life' (p. 107). But when Myrtle Wilson is run down and killed, her left breast is described, with no symbolic association at all, as a mangled feature of her lifeless body.

That capacity of a word to resonate with symbolic meaning or merely to represent a physical object is thematically important in this novel. Consider our response as readers to the name Gatsby: that word may expand to suggest the greatness of an American **archetype** with 'an extraordinary gift for hope' (p. 8); or it may contract to identify a bootlegger, or a man in love with another man's wife; or it may shrink still further to stand in a newspaper report for the lifeless victim of a violent crime.

Although he later modifies his judgement, Nick intially tells us that Gatsby 'represented everything for which I have an unaffected scorn' (p. 8). Meyer Wolfshiem describes Gatsby as 'the kind of man you'd like to take home and introduce to your mother and sister' (p. 70). Henry Gatz says of his son, 'If he'd of lived, he'd of been a great man' (p. 160). Like the varying associations of that name, symbols in this novel may change their meaning according to the light in which they are cast or the **point of view** from which they are seen.

Study focus: Words and interpretations

For Jay Gatsby the green light at the end of the Buchanans' dock is a symbolic focus for his desire for Daisy. The colour green recurs numerous times in this novel, and as readers we may choose to link it with a range of symbolic associations: Nature, fertility, growth and lushness in the organic world; envy or jealousy; immaturity; or money – green being the colour of a dollar bill. *The Great Gatsby* is a novel that is vitally concerned with shifts of understanding, differing perspectives and a range of possible interpretation.

PROGRESS CHECK

Section One: Check your understanding

These short tasks will help you to evaluate your knowledge and skills level in this particular area.

1. List three or four key **narrative** techniques used by Fitzgerald.

2. Identify three significant words or images that recur in this novel, and briefly describe how their meaning alters according to the context.

3. Make a table listing reasons why this novel lends itself or does not lend itself to adaptation as a film.

4. What are the main ways in which *The Great Gatsby* corresponds to the tragedy genre? List three or four ways.

5. List four reasons why this novel might be considered an American **romance** rather than a work of **realism**.

6. Find three or four examples of the novel's thematic concern with time (past, present and future).

7. What is the significance of the title, *The Great Gatsby*? List three or four ways in which the title shapes your expectations, or prepares you for reading the story.

8. What is the role played by **dialogue** in Nick's narrative? Write a paragraph presenting your ideas.

9. List five words that Nick uses which you find obscure, or that do not occur in everyday conversation. Give a dictionary definition for each.

10. Identify three events or situations within the novel that might be interpreted as having symbolic significance.

Section Two: Working towards the exam

Choose one of the following three tasks which require longer, more developed answers:

1. '*The Great Gatsby* is ultimately a novel about Nick's desire to be a writer.' Do you agree?

2. 'Modern tragedy depicts an individual's struggle to maintain human dignity.' Consider *The Great Gatsby* in light of this statement.

3. Consider the importance of point of view in *The Great Gatsby* and any other American novel you have studied.

A01 **PROGRESS BOOSTER**

For each Section Two task, read the question carefully, select the key areas you need to address, and plan an essay of six or seven points. Write a first draft, giving yourself an hour to do so. Make sure you include supporting evidence for each point, including quotations.

Progress check (rate your understanding on a level of 1 – low, to 5 – high)	1	2	3	4	5
How the story develops within a framing narrative					
How dialogue contributes to characterisation					
How an individual text can modify our understanding of a genre					
The dramatic effect of the scenic method					
The use of vocabulary and imagery for poetic effect within a prose narrative					

CONTEXTS

Historical context

Mass society

In 1920, the national census showed that America was, for the first time, a predominantly urban nation, with more people living in cities than in the countryside. Some of the places classified as cities were actually fairly small towns, but nonetheless the trend towards an urban America was unmistakable.

The growth of population due to immigration from Europe, and the movement of African Americans from the South, where their families had been held in slavery until the Civil War, encouraged this rapid expansion of America's cities. America's population more or less doubled in the fifty years before *The Great Gatsby* was published.

Advertising and the mass market

In order to meet the basic requirements of this growing population, mass-production techniques were developed in factories. In 1913, Henry Ford first used an assembly line to produce his Model-T automobile, but the manufacturing technique was already well established in the production of other goods for the mass market.

Fitzgerald's novel was written against the background of this rapid growth in consumer products, most of which were standardised – they looked the same and served the same use. Standardisation seemed appropriate to a modern democracy, where all citizens could buy items for their convenience and comfort. Manufacturing companies and large stores based in big cities produced catalogues that enabled Americans living in remote areas to purchase goods by mail order.

The whole notion of advertising changed. Instead of just letting people know what was available, advertisers in the early twentieth century set out to persuade potential customers that they needed to buy a certain product. The techniques of persuasion familiar from current forms of advertising started to be developed. Products were given brand names to make them stand out and seem attractive. Packaging became much more important, and salesmen were trained in new marketing techniques.

Conspicuous consumption

The term 'conspicuous consumption' was coined by a social scientist named Thorstein Veblen (1857–1929). He was born in the American Midwest in 1857, and published a book in 1899 entitled *The Theory of the Leisure Class*. 'Conspicuous consumption' referred to the way in which some wealthy Americans displayed their wealth through their houses and possessions. Thorstein Veblen was critical of this kind of display, as it often seemed irresponsible, extravagant and wasteful.

KEY CONNECTION **A03**

The young women who attend Gatsby's parties, dancing and drinking, were displaying through their behaviour a newly acquired sense of independence and freedom. With these Jazz Age 'flappers' compare the depiction of strong and independent women in earlier novels such as Dreiser's *Sister Carrie* (1900) or Willa Cather's *My Ántonia* (1918).

The Great Gatsby presents some very obvious illustrations of conspicuous consumption. Tom Buchanan, who is certainly a member of the leisure class, so wealthy that he does not need to work, has a team of polo ponies which he takes with him on his travels. He seems to keep them in part as a status symbol.

Jay Gatsby has his mansion, lavish parties, cars, motorboats and a new hydroplane. The flamboyance of his lifestyle is remote from the dusty world inhabited by George Wilson. But their worlds collide in the accident that kills Myrtle, and the fact that Gatsby has an expensive and easily identifiable car, a blatant example of conspicuous consumption, seals his fate.

Progress booster: Desire and vision

Note that desire and vision, two of the major thematic concerns in *The Great Gatsby*, are both important issues within the emerging consumer culture of 1920s America. Pay careful attention to the techniques Gatsby uses to persuade Daisy that he is the man she should desire. He needs to be seen as, in effect, he is selling himself through his impeccable well-tailored appearance, his expensive and imported possessions, and his lavish parties. Should we think of the novel as an account of a marketing campaign rather than a conventional love story?

The First World War

The First World War was fought between July 1914 and November 1918. For a few years America refused to take part in the conflict, but in April 1917 the president, Woodrow Wilson, declared that America would join forces with Great Britain, France and their allies against Germany and its allies. Nearly 3 million men were drafted into the American army and many of them were sent to Europe.

In this novel, Nick Carraway and Jay Gatsby are said to have been amongst those soldiers sent to fight in France. Nick mentions specifically the Battle of the Argonne Forest, an offensive in northern France near the end of the war. The American army suffered over 100,000 casualties in this battle, which lasted more than a month.

The Jazz Age

The decade following the First World War in America has become popularly known as the Jazz Age. Some very fine musicians were establishing jazz as an African-American art form during the 1920s, such as trumpeter Louis Armstrong (1901–71) and pianist and composer Duke Ellington (1899–1974). Yet wealthy young white audiences tended to like jazz not for the skill and imagination of these artists, but simply for dancing or as a soundtrack for wild behaviour.

The term 'the Jazz Age' was actually coined by Fitzgerald, whose fourth book and second collection of short stories, published in 1922, was entitled *Tales of the Jazz Age*. All the stories had previously appeared in newspapers or fashionable magazines such as *Vanity Fair*. The 1920s were also known at the time as the Golden Twenties or the Roaring Twenties. Fitzgerald portrayed these post-war years as a time of pleasure seeking and indulgence.

> **A01** **PROGRESS BOOSTER**
>
> Nick Carraway is writing his account in 1924, two years after the events of the story have occurred. Think carefully about the effect this distance in time has on his **narrative**. Do we learn anything about what he has done or what has happened to him in the intervening period?

The Lost Generation

Gertrude Stein, a remarkable American writer living in Paris, said that the First World War had produced a Lost Generation. The essence of this Lost Generation is captured brilliantly in *The Sun Also Rises* (1926), by Fitzgerald's close friend Ernest Hemingway. Hemingway's characters wander aimlessly through Europe, feeling emotionally empty. Fitzgerald had already captured this sense of exhaustion and pointlessness when he wrote, at the end of his first novel *This Side of Paradise* (1920), of a new generation 'grown up to find all Gods dead, all wars fought, all faiths in man shaken'.

Prohibition and organised crime

There is a lot of alcohol consumed in *The Great Gatsby*. Yet it is set during a time when the manufacture and distribution of alcoholic drinks were prohibited in America. This Prohibition commenced on 16 January 1920. Prohibition, championed by the Anti-Saloon League, was intended to raise the nation's moral standards, but to a large extent it had the opposite effect. It was difficult to enforce, as Fitzgerald's novel makes very clear.

It has been estimated that in 1925 there were around one hundred thousand speakeasies – illegal drinking dens – in New York City alone. Bootlegging, the illicit production and supply of alcohol, made rapid fortunes for criminals such as the gangster Al Capone. Bootlegging appears to be a major source of Gatsby's wealth. Prohibition was eventually repealed in 1933.

Organised crime, run by powerful gangsters, was a violent reality in American cities such as New York and Chicago during the 1920s. Actual criminals such as Al Capone, 'Lucky' Luciano, Dutch Schultz and 'Legs' Diamond provided models for the popular gangster movies of the 1930s such as *Little Caesar* (1930), *Public Enemy* (1931) and *Scarface* (1932). Their celebrity did not conceal the fact that these were ruthless and extremely dangerous men. In *The Great Gatsby* this criminal underworld is represented by Meyer Wolfshiem, a character based on the real-life gambler Arnold Rothstein.

Revision task 11: Style and substance

In *The Great Gatsby*, America can be seen as a place where style is more important than substance.

Make notes outlining how you would use a particular critical theory (such as Feminism, Marxism, Ecocriticism or New Historicism) to examine this claim. A Feminist approach, for example, might start with Daisy's suggestion, 'that's the best thing a girl can be in this world, a beautiful little fool' (p. 22) and then look more generally at relationships between style and gender roles within the novel.

A revolution in time

In 1875, fifty years before Fitzgerald wrote *The Great Gatsby*, passengers on a train travelling from New York on the East coast to San Francisco on the West, would have needed to change their watches around 200 times in order to show the correct time in each of the towns they passed through. Time was still measured locally, rather than according to some global standard.

In 1884 a conference in Washington DC proposed that the exact length of each day should be fixed and that the world should be formally divided into twenty-four time zones, with the Royal Observatory at Greenwich (in south London), as the point from which these zones were calculated. This innovation occurred not least because improvements in rail travel created a need for a network of coordinated timetables.

The development of wireless telegraphy in the 1880s, allowing rapid communication over large distances, helped to make this practicable, although it was not until 1912 that an International Conference on Time, held in Paris, established procedures for using signals to regulate time measurement accurately around the world.

The incidents that lead to the death of Jay Gatsby occurred, in Fitzgerald's fictional account, in 1922. Globalised time was a new phenomenon. This may seem quite abstract, but coordinated time measurement had already played a key role in military organisation during the First World War, and in peacetime it was a crucial factor in the efficient day-to-day running of America's emerging mass society.

Fitzgerald was not alone amongst writers of the 1920s in showing an almost obsessive interest in the nature of time. *Mrs Dalloway*, published in 1925 by English novelist Virginia Woolf, is especially striking for the way it plays regulated, mechanically measured social time against the way time is experienced internally by an individual. *The Great Gatsby*, published just one month earlier, is comparable to Woolf's novel in its intense concern with memory and anticipation as unmeasurable aspects of our sense of time.

Jay Gatsby's awareness of the present is entangled with his recollection of the past and his dreams of the future in ways that can't be measured by the clock ticking on his washstand on page 95, or by the 'defunct mantelpiece clock' he nearly knocks to the floor on page 84. The net of Time so recently spread across the world cannot diminish Gatsby's belief in 'the orgastic future that year by year recedes before us' (p. 171).

Study focus: The shrinking of distance

A02

America is a large continent, at its widest around 2,750 miles from East to West coast. During Fitzgerald's lifetime the improvement of railways, but still more dramatically the rapid development of the motor car and the telephone network radically altered spatial relationships and that caused significant changes in social relationships. Journeys could be made far more quickly; communication over the phone was instantaneous. In effect distances appeared to shrink, or vanish altogether. Cars and telephones were both fairly recent inventions and in *The Great Gatsby* they are part of a relatively new world of human experience. Think carefully about the part played in this novel by such technological innovations.

Photography

Photographs of a crude kind were produced as far back as the 1820s. But photography improved from the late 1880s, not least because of innovations made by a young American bank clerk called George Eastman (1854–1932). He patented a new camera, using convenient strips of film rather than bulky plates, and coined the trademark Kodak. A craze for taking photographs soon followed, and in the 1920s photography was a popular hobby.

Some photos appeared in newspapers, magazines and advertisements during the 1920s, and played a role in that decade's involvement with image, glamour and celebrity. But the technology for photojournalism as we know it today didn't really develop until the 1930s.

A04 KEY CONNECTION

Fitzgerald responded to the emergence of mass society by creating 'The Great Gatsby', a character whose image makes him stand out from the crowd. Fitzgerald's contemporary the novelist John Dos Passos (1896–1970) recognised that modern cities tend to make individuals feel anonymous, even like cogs in a machine. He depicted this trend in *Manhattan Transfer* (1925), a novel about New York life, published in the same year as *The Great Gatsby*, which depicts multiple stories of collective life rather than focusing upon a single hero or central figure.

A03 KEY CONTEXT

Thomas Alva Edison (1847–1931), American inventor of the gramophone and the electric light bulb, also invented the motion-picture camera. Think carefully about the impact that these innovations in sight and sound must have had. Try to imagine how these really new media must have appeared to a novelist in the early twentieth century, communicating voice, character and action through the printed page.

The cinema

Since the early twentieth century, the American film industry has largely been based on the West coast, in and around Hollywood, California. At the time *The Great Gatsby* was written, films were still silent and in black and white, but they were nonetheless an extremely popular form of entertainment. The first film with sound, *The Jazz Singer*, was released in 1927, and a new era in cinema history began. Fitzgerald spent some time, later in his life, writing film scripts in Hollywood. He died there, leaving an unfinished novel, *The Last Tycoon*, about a film producer.

Jay Gatsby has the glamour of a movie star. That appearance is enhanced by the way his house and garden are lit. An actual movie director is present at Gatsby's party in Chapter 6, along with a female star, who is described as 'a gorgeous, scarcely human orchid of a woman' (p. 101).

Amusement parks

Amusement parks were the precursors of modern theme parks and usually featured all the attractions of the fun fair. They were extremely popular in America between the beginning of the twentieth century and the end of the 1920s, when a major downturn in the economy led to their decline. Steeplechase Park and Luna Park, located at Coney Island, New York, which is mentioned in *The Great Gatsby*, were still attracting vast crowds.

Settings

The action of *The Great Gatsby* takes place in New York, the major city on America's East coast. Nick Carraway works in the financial district, centred on Wall Street, in the Lower Manhattan district. Nick is a commuter and lives on the North Shore of Long Island, an actual island but still part of the New York metropolitan area.

Fitzgerald called the village where Nick and Gatsby live West Egg; the Buchanans live in East Egg. West Egg is based upon an actual place called King's Point, on the Great Neck Peninsula; East Egg is based upon Sands Point, a village on the Cow Neck Peninsula. These two peninsulas jut into a stretch of water called Long Island Sound, which is an estuary of the Atlantic Ocean. New York's East River runs into Long Island Sound.

George and Myrtle Wilson's home is in a 'valley of ashes' (p. 26) that seems to be based upon the Corona Ash Dumps, refuse tips for the city's waste, formerly located on the site of what is now a public park called Flushing Meadows.

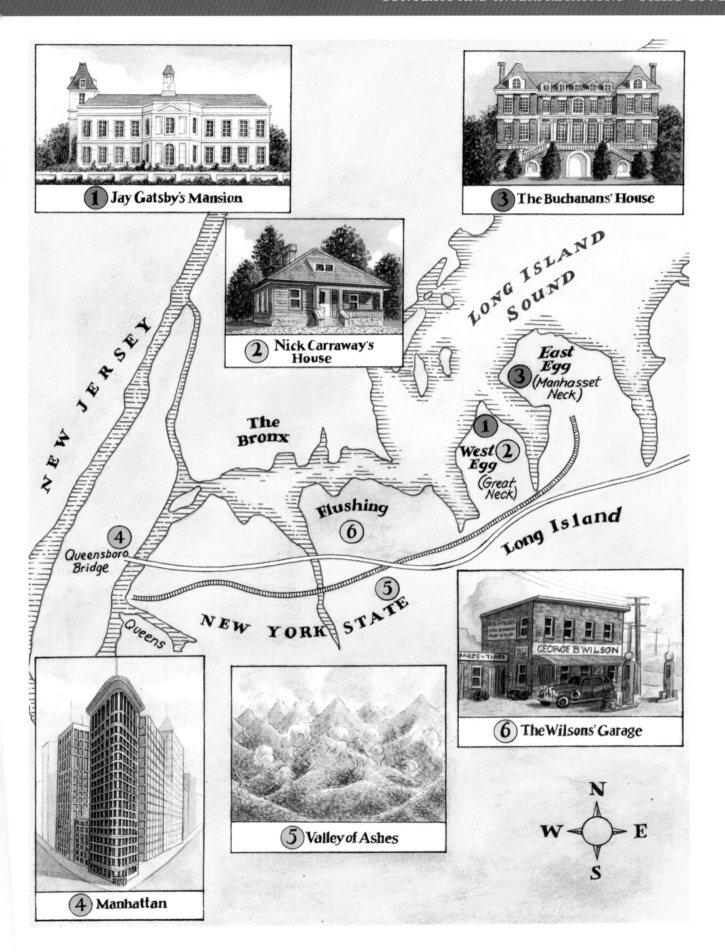

1 Jay Gatsby's Mansion

3 The Buchanans' House

2 Nick Carraway's House

East Egg (Manhasset Neck)

West Egg (Great Neck)

The Bronx

Flushing

Queensboro Bridge

Long Island

NEW JERSEY

LONG ISLAND Sound

NEW YORK STATE

Queens

6 The Wilsons' Garage

GEORGE B WILSON

5 Valley of Ashes

4 Manhattan

Literary context

Key influences

Joseph Conrad

Fitzgerald himself acknowledged that he had learnt a lot about **narrative** technique from reading the work of Polish-born, British novelist Joseph Conrad (1857–1924). Many of Conrad's books read like tales of adventure, and especially of life at sea; but Joseph Conrad saw the novel as a very serious art form, capable of responding to the complexity of the modern world. Joseph Conrad's novella *Heart of Darkness* (1902) and his novel *Lord Jim* (1900) had a notable influence upon Fitzgerald.

Joseph Conrad believed that there should be no word or phrase in a novel that does not contribute to its overall meaning. You can easily see from its intricate patterning that Fitzgerald shared Conrad's belief while he was writing *The Great Gatsby*. That concentration of meaning, with no wasted words, makes it a far more impressive novel than either *This Side of Paradise* or *The Beautiful and Damned*.

Fitzgerald followed the practice of Joseph Conrad, in *Lord Jim* and in *Heart of Darkness*, of making his **narrator** a participant in the story. As readers, we need to pay careful attention to the character of this narrator. We can't simply accept that he is giving us the truth in a detached and reliable way. Nick Carraway is deeply involved in the story he is telling, and in some respects he is an unreliable narrator.

Henry James

This important technical issue of narrative **point of view** was explored with great sophistication by Joseph Conrad's older friend, the American-born British novelist Henry James (1843–1916). Fitzgerald was also influenced by the scenic method he found in novels by Henry James, where a series of carefully constructed dramatic scenes with **dialogue** is embedded in the narrative, so that we almost feel we are watching a play (or a film) unfold.

The scenic method was also used in novels by Henry James's American friend, Edith Wharton. Fitzgerald sent her a copy of *The Great Gatsby*, and Edith Wharton said she thought his book was a masterly achievement.

T. S. Eliot

A number of critics have suggested that *The Great Gatsby* is indebted to T. S. Eliot's poem *The Waste Land* (1922). The debt seems to be more in terms of its portrayal of the 'valley of ashes' (p. 26) as a physically and spiritually desolate landscape, than a borrowing of technique or form. Fitzgerald did send a copy of the novel to T. S. Eliot, inscribed to the 'Greatest of Living Poets'.

The 'international theme'

T. S. Eliot (1888–1965), like Henry James, was an American who chose to live in England and acquired British nationality. Henry James actually made the comparison of Old World and New World cultures the central theme of his many novels and stories. He called it the 'international theme'. Fitzgerald picks up that theme in *The Great Gatsby*, weighing American against European values.

Contemporary American literature

Fitzgerald's novel handles themes and ideas that have recurred in American literary works since the start of the nineteenth century.

'The Custom House', Nathaniel Hawthorne's preface to his novel *The Scarlet Letter* (1850), contains the classic definition of American **romance**, a genre to which *The Great Gatsby* belongs. Hawthorne compares the effect of romance to that of moonlight illuminating a familiar room, transforming it into 'a neutral territory, somewhere between the real world and fairy-land, where the Actual and the Imaginary may meet, and each imbue itself with the nature of the other'. He felt that such a blend was especially well suited to depiction of life in the New World, where social life was far less well established and formalised than in Europe and in European novels.

Mark Twain recognised that romance could veer too far towards the Imaginary and away from the Actual. In *The Adventures of Huckleberry Finn* (1884) he makes trenchant criticism of such morally irresponsible tendencies in literature, escapist fantasies which Twain personified in the character Tom Sawyer. It may be useful to compare Gatsby's imaginative life with that of Tom Sawyer, and Nick's more down-to-earth perception of events with that of Huck Finn.

Walt Whitman's epic poem *Leaves of Grass* (1855) is a rapturous poetic statement of American egalitarian ideals. It contains 'Pioneer! O Pioneers!', a poem about the nation's westward expansion which supplied the title for Willa Cather's novel *O Pioneers!* (1913). Cather's account of the settlement of America's Middle West, the region in which James Gatz grew up, continued with *My Ántonia* (1918).

The relationship between Europe and the New World featured centrally in the novels of Henry James, who called it the 'international theme'. *The Great Gatsby* casts this theme in a particularly **ironic** light in the wake of the First World War. Ernest Hemingway's novel *A Farewell to Arms* (1929), set in Italy during that conflict, shows the collapse of Old World values and an American in search of some guideline as to how he should live.

Fitzgerald's interest in narrative point of view has a parallel in William Faulkner's *The Sound and the Fury* (1929), a technical tour de force of Modernist storytelling. Set in Mississippi, one of America's southern states, Faulkner's fiction is deeply entangled with racial attitudes and assumptions rooted in the violations and brutalities of the slave-holding past.

Richard Wright's *Native Son* (1940) is an African-American writer's powerful response to the kind of racist attitudes that surface in Tom Buchanan's dialogue in *The Great Gatsby*. The inequalities of wealth and class that Fitzgerald portrays might be compared with the depiction of New York's upper social strata in Edith Wharton's *The Age of Innocence* (1920) and the plight of the rural poor shown in John Steinbeck's *The Grapes of Wrath* (1939).

Fitzgerald's thematic treatment of desire which remains unfulfilled despite the attainment of material success may fruitfully be compared with Dreiser's characterisation of Carrie Meeber in *Sister Carrie* (1900).

Connections with love poetry

Fitzgerald's depiction of Gatsby's love for Daisy has an intensity, but also a complexity, that makes it highly suitable for comparison with a range of love poetry. Look, for example, at the techniques of persuasion in Marvell's 'To His Coy Mistress'; obsessive desire for a lost love in Dowson's 'Non sum qualis eram'; the ideal of Love transcending the passage of Time in Shakespeare's 'Sonnet 116'; the link between material prosperity and moral downfall in Hardy's 'The Ruined Maid'; or the chivalric imagery, sense of enchantment and subsequent desolation in Keats's 'La Belle Dame sans Merci'.

A03 **KEY CONTEXT**

It is possible that Fitzgerald chose to set his novel in 1922 in part because it was an important year in the development of literary modernism. T. S. Eliot's challenging poem *The Waste Land* was first published in that year. Its form, juxtaposing disparate fragments, resembles the collage forms used extensively in the visual arts during the early twentieth century.

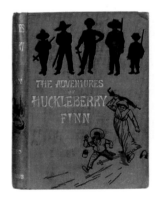

CRITICAL INTERPRETATIONS

F. Scott Fitzgerald's reputation

When F. Scott Fitzgerald died in 1940, his reputation as a writer was low. Obituaries tended to characterise him as an author who had failed to fulfil his early promise. He was working in Hollywood, as a scriptwriter, and had become an alcoholic. Some commentators suggested that his drinking problem resulted in flaws in his later writing.

In fact, early criticism tended to view Fitzgerald as the writer of numerous entertaining but rather lightweight stories, written primarily to make money and be published in magazines. The work he himself regarded as his real achievement, notably *The Great Gatsby*, tended to be overlooked.

A little over ten years later, Fitzgerald had become recognised as one of the major writers in the history of American literature. This change in his reputation was initially due to the efforts of literary critic Edmund Wilson (1895–1972), who secured publication in 1941 for *The Last Tycoon*, the novel Fitzgerald left unfinished, and in 1945 for a collection of Fitzgerald's essays, letters and notes entitled *The Crack-Up*.

Reaction on publication

The Great Gatsby received more favourable reviews than any of Fitzgerald's other books. Its positive critical reception was not matched by sales, but he received letters of praise from fellow writers including Gertrude Stein, Willa Cather and Edith Wharton, and from the poet T. S. Eliot, who thought it was the first significant advance in American fiction since Henry James.

Subsequent criticism

In 1945, the critic Lionel Trilling wrote an essay in which he suggested that Gatsby could be taken as a figure who represented America itself. In 1954, this insight was developed by Marius Bewley in another essay, 'Scott Fitzgerald's Criticism of America'.

The appearance of a series of biographies of Fitzgerald has encouraged some works of biographical criticism, in which certain people and events that provided Fitzgerald with raw material for his fiction are identified.

There have also been essays which have suggested literary influences on the writing of *The Great Gatsby*, notably Joseph Conrad's fiction, the poetry of T. S. Eliot and of John Keats, and a range of Christian and pagan myths. Other critics have focused upon Fitzgerald's language, and upon the formal aspects of the novel, especially the role of the **narrator**.

Contemporary approaches

A large number of critical books and essays on *The Great Gatsby* have now been published. Yet the novel continues to stimulate analysis. It is written in a rich and concentrated way, and lends itself to critical readings from a wide range of points of view. Literary critics adopt a variety of approaches. Their readings focus on different aspects on the novel, and this can result in radically differing interpretations.

Feminist criticism

Feminist criticism has been concerned to reveal how literary works have supported or challenged the assumptions of a male-dominated social order, often called a patriarchal society. There are numerous strands of Feminist criticism, but a basic approach might show us how the lives of characters in *The Great Gatsby* reflect patriarchal values, or suggest alternatives.

Tom Buchanan is clearly an embodiment of those patriarchal values. He likes to exercise power over women, even to treat them as his possessions. When Myrtle upsets him, Tom asserts his authority through violence and breaks her nose. Daisy often seems to have no will of her own and to follow helplessly in Tom's wake. When she does choose to exercise her will, visiting Gatsby's house, Tom gets angry and says, 'Nowadays people begin by sneering at family life and family institutions, and next they'll throw everything overboard and have marriage between black and white' (p. 124).

A Feminist critic might cite this as an example of how the traditional family unit in American society, dominated by the male's powerful role as husband and father, has constrained the lives of women, in their role as loyal wife and mother. In this outburst we can see how Tom's desire to maintain control spills over into overt racism.

A Feminist approach might also point out that Jay Gatsby's obsession with an idealised version of Daisy does nothing to help the actual woman to achieve her liberation. Indeed, Daisy is apparently driven still further into subservience to the domineering Tom Buchanan.

Marxist criticism

The philosopher Karl Marx (1818–83) suggested that history has involved a long struggle between social classes. He argued that the working class would eventually overthrow the wealthy ruling class, who exercise power and control the way daily life is led in a capitalist society. A Marxist literary critic might focus upon the lives of George and Myrtle Wilson, running a garage in the 'valley of ashes' (p. 26), in order to show how workers were oppressed in America during the 1920s.

The Wilsons are condemned by the economic system to remain poor, and to live in a bleak, unhealthy environment. The wealthy – who never seem to work – live in luxury, in houses that are compared to palaces, and behave like lords in the feudal society of the European Middle Ages. The rich seem to be trying to roll back time, to reverse the history of class struggle and go back to an earlier social order.

A Marxist approach might criticise Jay Gatsby for denying his working-class roots, for using criminal means to enter the ranks of the ruling class and for then behaving like a knight in an old-fashioned **romance**, with Daisy as the grail at the end of his quest. Gatsby's death might be seen, within this perspective, as the inevitable outcome of an individual directing all his energy into a purely personal fantasy, rather than engaging with the kind of social injustice that leaves people such as Tom Buchanan with power and leisure, while working people have to labour and suffer hardship.

 **KEY INTERPRETATION**

The Great Gatsby lends itself to a wide range of critical approaches. For example, an eco-critical reading might focus upon America's transformation from 'a fresh, green breast of the new world' (p. 171) to a modern industrial and urbanised society, and examine critically ways in which that change is reflected in the plot and characterisation as well as the settings of this novel. A post-colonial critic might focus upon the frequency of references in the novel to European tastes and values in order to disclose the persistence in America of Old World power and influence supposedly left behind in 1776, when Americans declared independence.

A05 **KEY INTERPRETATION**

Lois Tyson, in 'You Are What You Own: A Marxist Reading of *The Great Gatsby*', suggests that, while it portrays in a superficially appealing way the glamorous lifestyle of the wealthy, the novel is actually 'a scathing critique of American capitalist culture and the ideology that promotes it'. Tyson argues that Fitzgerald effectively depicts ways in which dedication to commodities (and the process of commodification) in this culture results in dysfunctional interpersonal and social relationships.

KEY CONNECTION **A04**

Fitzgerald's final completed novel, *Tender is the Night* (1934) deals directly with psychoanalysis as a theme, and draws heavily on the author's own life and his wife's struggle with schizophrenia. Fitzgerald could be said to use the novel as a way of working out his own present and past troubles, such as the alcoholism that would ultimately ruin his life.

KEY INTERPRETATION **A05**

Lois Tyson, in '"What's Love Got to Do with It?": A Psychoanalytic Reading of *The Great Gatsby*', views the novel as 'a drama of dysfunctional love'. Her approach focuses upon a fear of intimacy that inhibits relationships between Tom and Daisy, between Tom and Myrtle, between the Wilsons, and between Nick and Jordan. The prevailing fear is that the formation of emotional ties to another person will result inevitably in emotional devastation. The novel, seen in this light, is a tense account of unresolved psychological conflicts.

Psychoanalytic criticism

The neurologist Sigmund Freud (1856–1939) developed the discipline of psychoanalysis, which suggests that human behaviour is to a large extent determined by desires and drives of which we are unconscious. We may become aware of these desires and drives through indirect means such as dreams, or slips of the tongue.

A literary critic taking a psychoanalytic approach might point to the passage where we learn that, as a boy, Gatsby's 'heart was in a constant, turbulent riot. The most grotesque and fantastic conceits haunted him in his bed at night' (p. 95). In these waking dreams, Gatsby tussles with unconscious desires that he can't really grasp.

The physical realities of his boyhood, growing up on a farm in the Midwest with ordinary parents, didn't live up to the power of these desires, so Gatsby left his parents and severed contact with them. By erasing his parents in this way, Gatsby was psychologically releasing himself to be born again. Meeting Daisy, he was introduced to a previously unknown way of life that in certain ways matched his unconscious desires. His obsession with Daisy became a means to bring into existence the person he himself longed to be.

Nick tells us that Gatsby 'knew that when he kissed this girl, and forever wed his unutterable visions to her perishable breath, his mind would never romp again like the mind of God' (p. 107). In this psychoanalytic reading, then, Daisy is not in herself the object of Gatsby's desire; she is just one more stage prop in his inner drama. Gatsby's love is actually self-love; he is driven by a powerful unconscious desire to become 'The Great Gatsby'. In his attempt to become this fantasy self, he destroys James Gatz, destroys his parents and eventually destroys Jay Gatsby too.

New Historicist criticism

'New Historicism', a term coined by critic Stephen Greenblatt, approaches literary texts not as privileged works of art that stand outside of history but as documents that may be read in conjunction with non-literary texts in order to produce critical understanding of particular historical moments and cultural contexts.

A New Historicist reading of *The Great Gatsby* would recognise that the novel, as well as Fitzgerald, its author, was embedded within the social and economic realities of American life at the time of its writing. Such a reading might aim to reveal how the text came to be shaped by particular attitudes or assumptions, or it might use the text to shed light on social relationships or to analyse the exercise of power within 1920s America.

A New Historicist critic might, for example, examine the novel in relation to the text of *American Individualism*, a pamphlet published by Herbert Hoover, president of the United States, in 1922, the year in which the action of *The Great Gatsby* takes place. Hoover's argument was that America has a social system of its own, based upon a kind of individualism quite different from that found in the Old World. Hoover contrasted the success of the American system with the flawed societies of Europe, recently disrupted dramatically by war and revolution. Fitzgerald's novel might be read in the light of this political statement, but it might also be used to help make an analysis of Hoover's text.

PROGRESS CHECK

Section One: Check your understanding

These short tasks will help you to evaluate your knowledge and skills level in this particular area.

1. List three forms of technology that play a significant role in the story of *The Great Gatsby*. Include a brief description of the role played by each.

2. What kind of insights might be gained from a post-colonial reading of *The Great Gatsby*? Write a paragraph outlining your ideas.

3. List four to five events or situations that might provide focal points for a feminist reading of this novel. Briefly describe the significance of each for such a reading.

4. '*The Great Gatsby* is a novel of the Lost Generation.' List three events or details that support that claim.

5. Write a paragraph outlining what you understand by the term 'literary modernism'. Include specific reference to *The Great Gatsby*.

6. What kind of insights might be gained from a New Historicist reading of *The Great Gatsby*? Write a paragraph outlining your ideas.

7. Make a table listing at least five points of connection between *The Great Gatsby* and another literary text you have studied.

8. In what ways does *The Great Gatsby* register the fact that by the early 1920s America was becoming a mass society? List four to five ways.

9. Identify three actual historical events that are referred to in the novel and comment briefly on their significance within Nick's **narrative**.

10. Make a table contrasting four key characteristics of the world in which James Gatz grew up and the world in which the adult Jay Gatsby lived.

Section Two: Working towards the exam

Choose one of the following three tasks which require longer, more developed answers:

1. Examine the roles of George and Myrtle Wilson using three different critical approaches (e.g. eco-critical, Feminist, New Historicist).

2. 'We see the American 1920s through the eyes of Doctor Eckleburg.' How would you interpret this statement?

3. Consider the significance of technology in *The Great Gatsby* and in any other American novel.

A01 **PROGRESS BOOSTER**

For each Section Two task, read the question carefully, select the key areas you need to address, and plan an essay of six or seven points. Write a first draft, giving yourself an hour to do so. Make sure you include supporting evidence for each point, including quotations.

Progress check (rate your understanding on a level of 1 – low, to 5 – high)	1	2	3	4	5
How some knowledge of context enhances interpretation of the novel					
The different ways the novel can be read, according to critical approaches such as Marxist or post-colonial					
How comparison with another literary work can deepen understanding of both					
How a reader's interpretation may differ from the author's intended meaning					
How *The Great Gatsby* may be read as a historical document					

ASSESSMENT FOCUS

How will you be assessed?

Each particular exam board and exam paper will be slightly different, so make sure you check with your teacher exactly which Assessment Objectives you need to focus on. You are likely to get more marks for Assessment Objectives 1, 2 and 3, but this does not mean you should discount 4 or 5. Bear in mind that if you are doing AS Level, although the weightings are the same, there will be no coursework element.

What do the AOs actually mean?

	Assessment Objective	Meaning
AO1	Articulate informed, personal and creative responses to literary texts, using associated concepts and terminology, and coherent, accurate written expression.	You write about texts in accurate, clear and precise ways so that what you have to say is clear to the marker. You use literary terms (e.g. 'simile') or refer to concepts (e.g. 'the American Dream') in relevant places. You do not simply repeat what you have read or been told, but express your own ideas based on in-depth knowledge of the text and related issues.
AO2	Analyse ways in which meanings are shaped in literary texts.	You are able to explain in detail how the specific techniques and methods used by Fitzgerald to create the text (e.g. **narrative** voice, **dialogue**, **metaphor**) influence and affect the reader's response.
AO3	Demonstrate understanding of the significance and influence of the contexts in which literary texts are written and received.	You can explain how the text might reflect the social, historical, political or personal backgrounds of Fitzgerald or the time when the novel was written. You also consider how *The Great Gatsby* might have been received differently over time.
AO4	Explore connections across literary texts.	You are able to explain links between *The Great Gatsby* and other texts, perhaps of a similar genre, or with similar concerns, or viewed from a similar perspective (e.g. Feminist).
AO5	Explore literary texts informed by different interpretations.	You understand how *The Great Gatsby* can be viewed in different ways, and are able to write about these debates, forming your own opinion. For example, how a critic might view Gatsby as a corrupt symbol of a decaying America, whilst another might see him as representative of a tragic ideal which is ultimately optimistic.

What does this mean for your revision?

Whether you are following an AS or A Level course, use the right-hand column above to measure how confidently you can address these objectives. Then focus your revision on those aspects you feel need most attention. Remember, throughout these Notes, the AOs are highlighted, so you can flick through and check them in that way.

Next, use the tables on page 85. These help you understand the differences between a satisfactory and an outstanding response.

Then, use the guidance from page 86 onwards to help you address the key AOs, for example how to shape and plan your writing.

Features of **mid-level** responses: the following examples relate to Nick's role in the novel:

	Features	Examples
A01	You use critical vocabulary appropriately for most of the time, and your arguments are relevant to the task, ordered sensibly, with clear expression. You show detailed knowledge of the text.	*Nick is both **narrator** and writer in Chapter 3 as he **recollects** the events of Gatsby's parties. This means it is his **perspective** through which the story is told.*
A02	You show straightforward understanding of the writer's methods, such as how form, structure and language shape meanings.	*Nick's role is also that of a **spectator**. This **has the effect** of both **distancing** the reader, **so that** we can **judge** what happens, and **drawing** the reader in.*
A03	You can write about a range of contextual factors and make some relevant links between these and the task or text.	*The **idea of 'the Frontier'** – the pioneering spirit – is important in the novel, but Nick goes East rather than West, the opposite way to the pioneers.*
A04	You consider straightforward connections between texts and write about them clearly and relevantly to the task.	*Nick refers to a family tradition that the Carraways are descended from Scottish dukes. This idea surfaces in other American works, including Fitzgerald's short stories, **such as 'The Ice Palace'** in which Sally Carrol is acutely aware of the differences between herself and her fiancé's family.*
A05	You tackle the debate in the task in a clear, logical way, showing your understanding of different interpretations.	*Some would argue that Nick's role is a passive one, **but it could equally be said that he enables Gatsby to reconnect with Daisy**, so we could see him as having actively affected the course of the narrative.*

Features of a **high-level** response: these examples relate to a task on narrative perspectives:

	Features	Examples
A01	You are perceptive, and assured in your argument in relation to the task. You make fluent, confident use of literary concepts and terminology; and express yourself confidently.	*The novel is one in which perspectives constantly shift, even if, superficially, it is through a single lens – Nick's – that we see events. Indeed, Tom's view of Gatsby is **integral** both to the **narrative action** and to the **way we see** both men. It could even be argued that Tom sees Gatsby through a more truthful lens than Nick.*
A02	You explore and analyse key aspects of Fitzgerald's use of form, structure and language and evaluate perceptively how they shape meanings.	*The narrative, as it is **filtered** for us through Nick's eyes, **moves from the immediate** – for example, in the dialogue about Daisy's bruised finger in Chapter 1 – **to a more distant overview** in which Nick draws conclusions – for example saying, 'It [the evening] was sharply different from the West …' In this way, Fitzgerald constantly shifts our focus.*
A03	You show deep, detailed and relevant understanding of how contextual factors link to the text or task.	*The **American Dream** and **the rise of industrial power** which led to increasing wealth towards the end of the nineteenth century and at the beginning of the twentieth are **reflected in different ways through Tom and Gatsby – one has real inherited wealth and the other pretends to.** Socio-economic factors also affect George Wilson, who lives under the shadow of the increasing gap between the haves and have-nots.*
A04	You show a detailed and perceptive understanding of issues raised through connections between texts. You have a range of excellent supportive references.	*Tragedy, in its classical incarnation in **works by Sophocles**, for example, proceeds from the actions of a great man brought down by a fundamental weakness. However, **the novel constantly interrogates the idea of Gatsby as 'great'**: indeed, it may even be meant **ironically**. And is his love for Daisy weakness, or the thing that redeems him?*
A05	You are able to use your knowledge of critical debates and the possible perspectives on an issue to write fluently and confidently about how the text might be interpreted.	*Daisy could be viewed as passive, despite her avowal that she's 'been everywhere and seen everything and done everything'. In **feminist theory** terms, she has become **'objectified'**, and reduced to little more than her husband's possession. It might even be argued that Gatsby and Nick, too, reduce her to an idea of feminine loveliness.*

HOW TO WRITE HIGH-QUALITY RESPONSES

The quality of your writing – how you express your ideas – is vital for getting a higher grade, and **AO1** and **AO2** are specifically about **how** you respond.

Five key areas

The quality of your responses can be broken down into **five** key areas.

> **EXAMINER'S TIP**
>
> AO1 and AO2 are equally important in AS and A Level responses.

1. The structure of your answer/essay

- First, get **straight to the point in your opening paragraph**. Use a sharp, direct first sentence that deals with a key aspect and then follow up with evidence or detailed reference.
- **Put forward an argument** or **point of view** (you won't **always** be able to challenge or take issue with the essay question, but generally, where you can, you are more likely to write in an interesting way).
- **Signpost your ideas** with connectives and references which help the essay flow. Aim to present an overall argument or conceptual response to the task, not a series of unconnected points.
- **Don't repeat points already made**, not even in the conclusion, unless you have something new to add.

Aiming high: Effective opening paragraphs

Let's imagine you have been asked about the role of **narrators** in tragedies. Here's an example of a successful opening paragraph:

Gets straight to the point

The extent to which the reader can empathise with the tragic heart of the story is partly dependent on Nick's reliability as a narrator. When he remarks that Gatsby 'represented everything for which I have an unaffected scorn', he not only sets up a critical tension between his judgement and the novel's title, but in making that remark he calls into question his opening assertion that he tends to reserve judgement. How then are we to view his later statements about Gatsby? Does Nick's involvement in the story heighten or diminish our sense of its tragic qualities?

Sets up some interesting ideas that will be tackled in subsequent paragraphs

2. Use of titles, names, etc.

This is a simple, but important, tip to stay on the right side of the examiners.

- Make sure that you spell correctly the titles of the texts, chapters, authors and so on. Present them correctly too, with inverted commas and capitals as appropriate. For example, 'The Great Gatsby'.
- Use the **full title**, unless there is a good reason not to (e.g. it's very long).
- Use the term 'text' rather than 'book' or 'story'. If you use the word 'story', the examiner may think you mean the plot/action rather than the 'text' as a whole.

3. Effective quotations

Do not 'bolt on' quotations to the points you make. You will get some marks for including them, but examiners will not find your writing very fluent.

The best quotations are:

- Relevant and not too long (you are going to have to memorise them, so that will help you select shorter ones!)
- Integrated into your argument/sentence
- Linked to effect and implications

Aiming high: Effective use of quotations

Here is an example of an effective use of a quotation about social class in the novel:

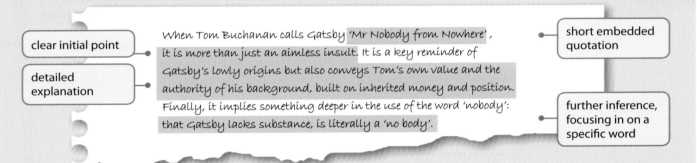

Remember – quotations can also be one or two single words or phrases embedded in a sentence to build a picture or explanation, or they can be longer ones that are explored and picked apart.

4. Techniques and terminology

By all means mention literary terms, techniques, conventions, critical theories or people (for example, 'paradox', **'archetype'**, 'feminism' or 'Plato') **but** make sure that you:

- Understand what they mean
- Are able to link them to what you're saying
- Spell them correctly

5. General writing skills

Try to write in a way that sounds professional and uses standard English. This does not mean that your writing will lack personality – just that it will be authoritative.

- Avoid colloquial or everyday expressions such as 'got', 'alright', 'ok' and so on.
- Use terms such as 'convey', 'suggest', 'imply', 'infer' to explain the writer's methods.
- Refer to 'we' when discussing the audience/reader.
- Avoid assertions and generalisations; don't just state a general point of view ('Nick Carraway's narration cannot be taken at face value because it is flawed'), but analyse closely with clear evidence and textual detail.

Note the professional approach here in the choice of vocabulary and awareness of the effect on the reader:

Fitzgerald **conveys** *the sense of a society struck by a malaise, drifting towards its ruin while the party still goes on. As readers* **we** *feel a sense of decay and decadence as the chapter progresses.*

QUESTIONS WITH STATEMENTS, QUOTATIONS OR VIEWPOINTS

One type of question you may come across is one that includes a statement, quotation or viewpoint from another reader. You are likely to be asked this about *The Great Gatsby* and another text you have studied, but it won't be a comparison, so we will deal just with *The Great Gatsby* here.

These questions ask you to respond to, or argue for/against, a specific **point of view** or critical interpretation. This is likely to be in relation to the genre of tragedy, or in relation to a key theme of American literature.

For *The Great Gatsby* these questions will typically be like this:

> **'At the core of the tragic experience is a sense of disillusionment and decay.' To what extent do you agree with this view in relation to the two texts you have studied, bearing in mind the ways the writers have constructed their texts?**

The key thing to remember is that you are being asked to **respond to a particular perspective or critical view** of the text – in other words, to come up with **your own** 'take' on the idea or viewpoint in the task.

Key skills required

The table below provides help and advice on answering the question above.

Skill	Means?	How do I achieve this?
To focus on the specific aspect related to the tragic genre	You must show your understanding of tragedy as a genre which writers use, first tackling whether 'disillusionment' and 'decay' are key elements of tragedy, secondly deciding the degree to which they apply to the novel.	You will need to deal with the issue generally, either in an opening paragraph or in several paragraphs, but also make sure you keep on coming back to this issue throughout the essay, rather than diverting into other areas which you have not been asked about.
To consider different interpretations	There will be more than one way of looking at the given question. For example, critics might be divided about the extent to which Nick becomes disillusioned by what happens.	Show you have considered these different interpretations in your answer. For example, a student might write: *Nick prefers to identify the East coast as a place of distorted vision, where truth is corrupted, rather than allow himself to become disillusioned with his hero, Gatsby. Nick remains a loyal friend to the end.*
To write with a clear, personal voice	Your own 'take' on the question is made obvious to the examiner. You are not just repeating other people's ideas, but offering what **you** think.	Although you may mention different perspectives on the task, you settle on your own view. Use language that shows careful, but confident, consideration. For example: *Although it has been said that Nick Carraway is an unreliable narrator, I feel that a more fundamental issue is that truth itself cannot be disentangled from Nick's point of view.*
Construct a coherent argument	The examiner or marker can follow your train of thought so that your own viewpoint is clear to him or her.	Write in clear paragraphs that deal logically with different aspects of the question. Support what you say with well-selected and relevant evidence. Use a range of connectives to help 'signpost' your argument. For example: *We might say that Nick becomes disillusioned by Gatsby. However, he says early on in his narrative that Gatsby 'turned out alright at the end'. Moreover, it is through the writing of that narrative that Gatsby's memory is preserved and honoured.*

Answering a 'viewpoint' question

Let us look at another question:

> 'Tragedies are dependent on the idea that the central protagonist cannot avoid his or her fate.' To what extent do you agree with this view in relation to the two texts you have studied, bearing in mind the ways the writers have constructed their texts?

Stage 1: Decode the question

Underline/highlight the **key words**, and make sure you understand what the statement, quote or viewpoint is saying. In this case:

'**To what extent do you agree …**' means: *Do you wholly agree with this statement or are there aspects of it that you would dispute?*

'**Tragedies … dependent on …**' means: *The nature of tragedies is determined by …*

'**central protagonist**' means: *leading character in the story*

'**cannot avoid his or her fate**' means: *is powerless to alter the course of events*

So you are being asked whether you agree/disagree with *the view that every tragedy necessarily involves a significant figure who becomes a victim of circumstances.*

Stage 2: Decide what your viewpoint is

Examiners have stated that they tend to reward a strong view which is clearly put. Think about the question – can you take issue with it? Disagreeing strongly can lead to higher marks, provided you have **genuine evidence** to support your point of view. Don't disagree just for the sake of it.

Stage 3: Decide how to structure your answer

Pick out the key points you wish to make, and decide on the order that you will present them in. Keep this basic plan to hand while you write your response.

Stage 4: Write your response

Begin by expanding on the aspect or topic mentioned in the task title. In this way, you can set up the key ideas you will explore. For example:

Classical Greek and Shakespearean tragedy portrays the downfall of some noble figure, due to a flaw in their character or an error of judgement. It could be argued that this is the case in The Great Gatsby, *although as readers we have to take into account the complication that our knowledge of Gatsby is filtered through Nick's narration …*

Then in the remaining paragraphs proceed to set out the different arguments or perspectives, including your own.

In the final paragraph, end with a clear statement of your viewpoint, but do not list or go over the points you have made. End succinctly and concisely.

Then, proceed to dealing with the second text in a similar way.

COMPARING *THE GREAT GATSBY* WITH OTHER TEXTS

As part of your assessment, you may have to compare *The Great Gatsby* with or link it to other texts you have studied. These may be other novels, plays or even poetry. You may also have to link or draw in references from texts written by critics.

Linking or comparison questions might relate to a particular theme or idea, such as 'love'. For example:

> **By exploring the writers' methods, compare ideas about the emotional intensity generated by love in one prose text and one poetry text you have studied.**

Or:

> **Much American literature explores the theme of self-reinvention. By comparing *The Great Gatsby* with at least one other text prescribed for this topic, discuss how far you agree with this view.**

You will need to:

Evaluate the issue or statement and have an **open-minded approach**. The best answers suggest meaning**s** and interpretation**s** (plural):

- For example, in relation to the first question: do you agree that love is presented in this way? Is this aspect more important in one text than in another? Why? How?
- What are the different ways in which this question or aspect can be read or viewed?
- What evidence is there in each text for this perspective? How can you present it in a thoughtful, reflective way?
- What are the points of similarity and difference?

Express **original or creative approaches** fluently:

- This isn't about coming up with entirely new ideas, but you need to show that you're actively engaged with thinking about the question, not just reeling off things you have learnt.
- **Synthesise** your ideas – pull ideas and points together to create something fresh.
- This is a linking/comparison response, so ensure that you guide your reader through your ideas logically, clearly and with professional language.

Know **what** to compare/contrast: the writer's methods – **form, structure** and **language** – will **always** be central to your response. Consider:

- The authorial perspective or voice (who is speaking/writing), standard versus more conventional narration (use of flashback, **foreshadowing**, disrupted time or **narrative** voice which leads to dislocation or difficulty in reading)
- Different characteristic use of language (length of sentences, formal/informal style, dialect, accent, balance of **dialogue** and narration; difference between prose treatment of an idea and poem)
- Variety of symbols, images, motifs (how they represent concerns of author/time; what they are and how and where they appear; how they link to critical perspectives; their purposes, effects and impact on the narration)
- Shared or differing approaches (to what extent do Fitzgerald and the author(s) of Text 2/3 conform to/challenge/subvert approaches to writing about love?)

EXAMINER'S TIP

Remember that in order to score highly in your answer you will also need to discuss what the critics say (AO5) and consider relevant cultural or contextual factors (AO3).

Writing your response

Let us use the example from page 90:

> **By exploring the writers' methods, compare ideas about the emotional intensity generated by love in one prose text and one poetry text you have studied.**

EXAMINER'S TIP

If you are following an AS course, you may have less exam time to write than for the A level – so concise, succinct points with less elaboration than provided here may be needed.

Introduction to your response

- Either discuss quickly what 'emotionally intense relationships' means, and how well this applies to *The Great Gatsby* and two poems you have studied, or start with a particular moment from one of the texts which allows you to launch your exploration.

- For example, you could begin with a powerful quotation to launch your response:

'I've just heard the most amazing thing', Jordan Baker whispers to Nick Carraway in Chapter 3 of 'The Great Gatsby'. The 'amazing thing' she has heard is that Jay Gatsby has bought his huge mansion on West Egg simply because he wanted to live across the bay from Daisy Buchanan. Nick suddenly realises that Gatsby's extravagant house, his parties and possessions have a single purpose; they express Gatsby's intense feelings for the girl he fell in love with five years earlier.

Main body of your response

- **Point 1**: continue your exploration of one intense relationship in *The Great Gatsby*: what it implies about society, how Fitzgerald fitted it to the issues of the time, why this was/was not 'interesting' for readers at the time, and readers now. How might we interpret that relationship differently through time?

- **Point 2**: now cover a new factor or aspect through comparison or contrast of this relationship with another in Text 2 and/or 3. For example, *Shakespeare, in 'Sonnet 116', argues that 'Love is not Time's fool', but remains constant despite physical changes or altered circumstances*. How is/are the new relationship(s) in Text 2 presented **differently or similarly** by the writer according to language, form, structures used; why was this done in this way?

- **Points 3, 4, 5, etc.**: address a range of other factors and aspects, for example other 'intense' relationships **either** within *The Great Gatsby* **or** in both *The Great Gatsby* and the two poems. What different ways do you respond to these (with more empathy, greater criticism, less interest) – and why? For example:

Myrtle Wilson has also become attached to Tom Buchanan in a way that appears emotionally intense. Her feelings for him are so strong that she has come to despise her husband George, and wants to leave him and marry Tom. But Tom's appeal for Myrtle is primarily his wealth. She says that when they first met, during a train journey, 'he had on a dress suit and patent leather shoes, and I couldn't keep my eyes off him ….' Tom's clothes fascinated her. Fitzgerald presents their relationship as essentially shallow: Myrtle wants to escape her current way of life and experience the lifestyle of the rich, and this may make us think again about Gatsby's feelings for Daisy, whose lifestyle opens up a comparably new world for him. We need to ask whether Gatsby's emotional intensity is a form of self-absorption, or love for his own self-image, rather than genuine feeling for Daisy.

Conclusion

- Synthesise elements of what you have said into a final paragraph that fluently, succinctly and inventively leaves the reader/examiner with the sense that you have engaged with this task and the texts.

In 'Sonnet 116' love endures, 'an ever-fixèd mark / That looks on tempests and is never shaken' and that kind of durability, arising out of intense passion, is also found in Dowson's 'Non sum qualis eram'. However, in 'The Great Gatsby' the green light that seems to be the 'ever- fixèd mark' of Gatsby's passion is ultimately no more than a marker of Tom's property. After Gatsby's death it continues to shine as before, indifferent to the intensity of his dreams.

USING CRITICAL INTERPRETATIONS AND PERSPECTIVES

What is a critical interpretation?

The particular way a text is viewed or understood can be called an interpretation, and can be made by literary critics (specialists in studying literary texts), reviewers, or everyday readers and students. It is about taking a position on particular elements of the text, or on what others say about it. For example, you could consider:

1. Notions of 'character'

What **sort/type** of person Gatsby – or another character – is:

- Is the character an '**archetype**' (a specific type of character with common features)? The critic Paul A. Scanlon has suggested that Jay Gatsby is presented as a chivalric knight, and that his courtship of Daisy conforms to the conventions of medieval courtly love.
- Does the character personify, symbolise or represent a specific idea or trope ('the American Dream'?; 'the tragic hero'?)?
- Is the character modern, universal, of his/her time, historically accurate etc.? (For example, can we see aspects of today's celebrities in Gatsby? Does the way he cultivates his image resemble the way pop icons are presented through the media? Is he establishing a brand, as in a modern advertising campaign?)

2. Ideas and issues

What the novel tells us about **particular ideas or issues** and how we interpret these. For example:

- How society is structured: the American democratic ideal of equality of opportunity is seen to be frustrated in *The Great Gatsby* by the clear divisions of social class. This raises broader issues concerning relationships with the past and the exercise of power in post-colonial societies.
- The role of men/women: in the years following the First World War, young women in America behaved in a far more liberated way than earlier generations. But the novel shows that a patriarchal, male-dominated social order remains in place. Arguably Daisy is reduced to the status of an object through the action of Gatsby's obsessive gaze.
- Moral codes and social justice: criminal behaviour plays a significant role in this novel, but there are also indications that such behaviour is due, in part at least, to injustice and inequality, along lines of race and gender as well as social class.

3. Links and contexts

To what extent the novel **links with, follows or pre-echoes** other texts and/or ideas. For example:

- Gatsby's romantic view of reality, which often seems to resemble a kind of fantasy life, might be compared with Tom Sawyer's inability to see the world as it actually is and to develop appropriate moral awareness, in Twain's *The Adventures of Huckleberry Finn* (1884).
- The way Fitzgerald uses the American West in *The Great Gatsby* to represent the possibility of a new beginning might be compared with Willa Cather's depiction of Frontier life, in the challenging conditions of the unsettled Midwest, in *My Ántonia* (1918).
- In its frequent allusions to Old World values *The Great Gatsby* addresses what Henry James termed the 'international theme', as explored in his novel *The Portrait of a Lady* (1881).

4. Genre and narrative structure

How the novel is **constructed** and how Fitzgerald **makes** his narrative:

- Does it follow particular narrative conventions? For example, those of the tragic genre?
- What are the functions of specific events, characters, plot devices, locations etc. in relation to narrative or genre?
- What are the specific moments of tension, conflict, crisis and denouement – and do we agree on what they are?

5. Reader responses

How the novel **works on the reader**, and whether this changes over time and in different contexts:

- How does Fitzgerald **position** the reader? Are we to empathise with, feel distance from, judge and/or evaluate the events and characters?

6. Critical reaction

And, finally, how do different readers view the novel? For example, different critics over time, or different readers in the early 1920s in the US and in more recent years.

Writing about critical perspectives

The important thing to remember is that **you** are a critic too. Your job is to evaluate what a critic or school of criticism has said about the elements above, arrive at your own conclusions, and also express your own ideas.

In essence, you need to: **consider** the views of others, **synthesise** them, then decide on **your perspective**. For example:

Explain the viewpoints

Critical view A about America's potential:

An eco-critical reading of 'The Great Gatsby' might examine how the novel sheds light upon various ways in which the natural potential of the New World's 'fresh green breast' has been squandered in the process of urban development and industrialisation.

Critical view B about the same aspect:

A post-colonial reading might use 'The Great Gatsby' to shed light on ways in which the promise of a New World has been betrayed by the persistence of Old World values.

Then synthesise and add your perspective:

Valuable insights might be gained from the eco-critical argument that America, as depicted in 'The Great Gatsby', has transformed the natural world into artificial and degraded environments, and also from a post-colonial reading's focus upon the persistence of European values in American society. I think both suggest that America has failed to imagine its own future in a way that is radically different from the past. Jay Gatsby shares that flaw; he is unable to give form and meaning to his new life except through sentimental attachment to the past. In light of these critical readings, Jay Gatsby's individual fate can readily be interpreted as America's collective tragedy.

A05 KEY INTERPRETATION

Here are just two examples of different kinds of response to *The Great Gatsby*:

Critic 1 – Lois Tyson's 'Will the Real Nick Carraway Please Come Out?: A Queer Reading of *The Great Gatsby*', in her *Critical Theory Today*, argues that Nick is gay, although not consciously aware of his sexual orientation.

Critic 2 – Carlyle Van Thompson, in 'Jay Gatsby's Passing in F. Scott Fitzgerald's *The Great Gatsby*', argues that Fitzgerald characterises Gatsby as a 'pale' black individual who 'passes for white', i.e. is accepted socially as a white man.

ANNOTATED SAMPLE ANSWERS

Below are extracts from three sample answers at different levels to the same task/question. Bear in mind that these responses may not correspond exactly to the style of question you might face, but they will give a broad indication of some of the key skills required.

> 'Tragedies depend on a character whose central weakness prevents any chance of a happy conclusion: to what extent is this true of two of the texts you have studied?'

Candidate 1

A01 Clear opening, making specific reference to the text and weighing up possible readings

In order to say how true this statement is in relation to F. Scott Fitzgerald's 'The Great Gatsby' it is first necessary to find out what Gatsby's central weakness is. He is in love with Daisy, who is a married woman, but is that a weakness? Nick, who narrates the story, admires Gatsby's 'extraordinary gift for hope', so from that angle his hope to win Daisy's love is a strength rather than a weakness. The problem is that Gatsby has become a bootlegger in order to impress Daisy with his wealth and his glamorous lifestyle. We find out that he is a criminal and from that moment his downfall seems likely. But perhaps his downfall actually started when he first began to break the law.

A deeper problem is that he was born into a poor family, but that is not really his weakness. His unhappiness with the way his parents lived – 'shiftless and unsuccessful farm people' – might be seen as a strength. He wanted to improve his own life and Daisy represents the things he never knew at home, glamour and money. In real life, however, Daisy is not worthy of his love. She is cynical and superficial and a bad mother.

A01 Again, referring to details of text and weighing up pros and cons

A01 A basic point, but a sign of critical thinking

It is difficult to know what a happy conclusion to this story might have been. If Gatsby had his way, Daisy's relationship with Tom would come to an end, and this would disrupt their lives and that of their daughter Pammy. Even though their marriage is not a particularly happy one, with Tom committing adultery, it could scarcely be a happy ending for Daisy to leave him for a man who has links with the criminal underworld.

If Gatsby was more adaptable and found another person to love the story would not exist, and Nick would not have the achievement of writing a book. The situation of Gatsby buying expensive shirts and foreign cars to impress someone who already has a very wealthy husband is potentially a tragic one. But the central weakness doesn't seem to be part of his character. It is more the situation of trying to regain lost love.

A02 Awareness of another narrative level

A03 Relevant use of context, which might have been developed further

Although it is tragic that Gatsby dies, shot by George Wilson, it is important to bear in mind that a few years earlier millions of men had died in the First World War. You could say that war was tragic, although you could not blame it on a character who had a central weakness. In light of all those men dying Gatsby's death seems unimportant. Nick, who fought in the war, says that Gatsby

A01 Aware of different perspectives on textual details, but rather informal expression

represented 'everything for which I had an unaffected scorn'. That suggests that the reason he is telling his story is not because he regards him as a tragic hero. He does also say that Gatsby turned out ok in the end, which is another way of looking at him, but still not tragic.

Gatsby also represents America, in that a lot of his qualities – having hope, starting his life again, rising from rags to riches – are also American qualities. Is Fitzgerald saying that America is a tragic country? He does show that sexism and racism exist in the novel, and there is a huge gap between the lifestyle of the well-off, on West and East Egg, and the poor hard-working people, such as Gatsby's parents on their farm in the Middle West and the Wilsons, who live in a 'valley of ashes'. When I read the novel, however, I did not think of Gatsby as America, because he seems too wrapped up in his own world, which is basically his obsession with Daisy.

A01 Good, basic critical approach; aware of relevant issues and making sound broad judgements

Perhaps obsession is his central weakness. If only he could have moved on or changed the way he looked at things he might have lived. But when we see him at his parties he is aloof and doesn't mix. He is there to be seen rather than to form meaningful relationships. Nick is really the only friend he has, apart from Wolfshiem who is a gangster and a bad influence, although Wolfshiem does say that Gatsby is the sort of man you would like to introduce to your mother and sister. On the other hand, by getting him together with Daisy, his second cousin once removed, Nick only makes matters worse.

A05 Needs developing, but basis of sound critical approach evident

In conclusion, to say that 'The Great Gatsby' is a tragic story because of Gatsby's central weakness is too simple. It is a novel with a lot of layers of meaning and the vocabulary is patterned to create links between the chapters. But it seems to be the situations that Gatsby finds himself in at different times in his life that are the problem. He is not really to blame. According to the definition in the question I would say that 'The Great Gatsby' is not a tragedy, even though Gatsby's death is tragic in an everyday sense of that word.

The student then goes on to discuss the question in relation to *Richard II*.

MID LEVEL

Comment

- AO1 A clear and methodical approach, consistently weighing up pros and cons in a basic but consistent way. Needs to push the analysis further to move it beyond broad observations, but fundamentals of critical reading are in place.
- AO2 Broad sense of ways in which meaning is shaped in *The Great Gatsby*. Closer attention to language and technique would have raised the level of the analysis.
- AO3 Makes reference to historical context but critical engagement with it needs further development.
- AO4 No connections with other texts in this part of the question.
- AO5 This answer is marked by basic yet consistent critical evaluation, which demonstrates awareness of point of view. Doesn't engage with more sophisticated critical perspectives.

To improve the answer:

- Pay closer attention to the way meaning may be shaped by use of language and literary techniques. (AO2)
- Engage more purposefully with relevant historical and literary contexts. (AO3/AO4)
- Develop a more sophisticated understanding of how critical interpretations might shed light on key issues.

Candidate 2

A04 Broad literary connection

By calling his novel 'The Great Gatsby', Fitzgerald was inviting us as readers to recognise that his book is a tragedy. Since the days of Ancient Greece, tragic drama has involved the downfall of a character, from greatness to suffering and, often, death. That downfall was usually due to a tragic weakness of character, or to a mistake made by the hero. Jay Gatsby is a man who seems to have it all in terms of material success, but he throws it all away. The way he does so reveals a flaw in his nature. When Nick points out to him, 'You can't repeat the past', Gatsby replies, 'Why of course you can!' That belief lies at the heart of his central weakness.

A02 Very useful quote; analysis needs development

A01 Astute point and accurate use of literary term

In a sense Nick does repeat the past, by turning it into a story. That is ironic. But the flesh and blood reality of Jay Gatsby cannot be brought back to life after he has been murdered by George Wilson. Nick understands that and his melancholy sense of growing old colours the narrative. Nick knows that you can't turn back the clock, and although he is only thirty he speaks as though he is older. He sees his own future as 'the promise of a decade of loneliness'. It may be that bleak sense of his own life and prospects that attracts Nick to the story of Gatsby's downfall.

A02 Useful engagement with Nick's point of view

A02 Insightful point; needs developing

Gatsby's tragic end comes about because he identifies Daisy as the personification of his past, even though she is now married to another man and has a daughter. The fact that Daisy seems shallow and unworthy of Gatsby's love makes his refusal to leave the past behind all the more ridiculous. It is as though he has put the past behind him once – when he changed his name from James Gatz and left his home in the Middle West and his parents – but he is unable to put the love he felt for Daisy Fay behind him. That weakness prevents a happy conclusion to the novel.

A04 Shrewd comparison within the text

A02 Alertness to Nick's role

Nick is Daisy's second cousin once removed but he does not hide the fact that she is a superficial person. This helps us to recognise that Gatsby was actually drawn to her lifestyle when he first met her. He became obsessed with the wealth and glamour she represented. But even when he has the trappings of wealth and glamour he doesn't really live in the present. His tragic weakness is to remain trapped in that moment in the past when they met and he was exposed to another way of living: 'He found her excitingly desirable.'

It is ironic that Gatsby's own past is the subject of much speculation amongst people who scarcely know him. He is alleged to have killed a man, and to have been a German spy during the war. Because the past is no longer real you can say whatever you like about it. Only when there is still evidence can the historical truth be uncovered. Even then historians vary in their interpretations. Some view the 1920s in America as the Jazz Age, a time of parties and heavy drinking; but it was also the time of Prohibition, when selling alcohol was against the law, and it was the age of the Lost Generation, people drifting through life aimlessly in the wake of the First World War.

A03 Awareness of context but could be more developed

AO2 Aware of Nick's role and complexity

Nick collects evidence about Gatsby and tells a story he believes to be true, but even so there are lots of questions still to be answered. For example, is Gatsby really 'great'? But also is Nick reliable? If the narrator can't be trusted then what can we really know about the past? And if Gatsby is not great can he really be called a tragic hero? Perhaps what Nick is telling us is just a reflection of his own obsessions. Perhaps Gatsby was just deluded and self-dramatising, in which case the lack of a happy conclusion is essentially his own fault.

How could this story have ended happily? Myrtle might have lived, gone West with her husband George and started a fresh life. Nick and Jordan might have formed a meaningful relationship. Tom and Daisy might have found ways to make their marriage happier and less patriarchal. But Gatsby, fixated on the past, stands no chance of finding happiness. In fact the only really satisfactory conclusion in this novel is that Nick has gone back home to the Middle West and has settled down to writing. In composing this story he has fulfilled a dream of being a writer. 'I was rather literary in college', he tells us. From the point of view of narrative theory it is possible to say that as a consequence of Gatsby's death Nick is able to fulfil his own desire to write a book. In light of that argument 'The Great Gatsby' is not a tragedy but the story of a dream fulfilled. We might conclude that the dream belonged to F. Scott Fitzgerald as well as to Nick Carraway.

AO2 Adapts the question in ways that allow reflection on the presence and role of Nick, which is not the obvious response

The student then goes on to discuss the question in relation to *Richard II*.

GOOD LEVEL

Comment

- AO1 Places emphasis on Nick's role in the novel, which might have been off the mark, but actually results in a pleasingly personal, if slightly less focused, response.
- AO2 The emphasis on Nick's role results in a series of useful observations on how meaning is shaped or coloured within the narrative.
- AO3 A broad sense of America during the 1920s.
- AO4 Helpful, if rather basic, opening link to Greek tragedy.
- AO5 A sense that different perspectives are invited by this text, with leanings towards (rather than real engagement with) narrative theory.

To improve the answer:

- Tighten the argument so it appears a thought-out and well-directed answer rather than a series of useful and more loosely related insights. (AO1)
- Make more focused reference to historical and literary contexts. (AO3/AO4)
- Sharpen the sense of how a critical perspective shapes the interpretation of a text. (AO5)

Candidate 3

A01 A strong and distinctively personal opening paragraph, establishing an angle to tackle the question

'If he'd of lived, he'd of been a great man', says Henry C. Gatz, following the death of his son. Gatz, an unsophisticated man as his faulty grammar indicates, imagines that James Gatz would have achieved greatness by contributing to America's development as a country. He compares him to James J. Hill, a Middle West tycoon who made a personal fortune by building a railway link to America's West coast. But James Gatz became Jay Gatsby, achieved wealth apparently through criminal means and sacrificed his potential to the obsessive pursuit of a married woman.

If 'The Great Gatsby' is a tragedy in the terms outlined in the question, then Gatsby's central weakness is sentimental attachment to the past, to the excitement of a youthful love affair, or to the glamour of the privileged lifestyle of Daisy Fay and her family in Louisville. There can be little doubt that Gatsby had certain abilities and the kind of charm that could have made him successful in the way his father envisaged. The way he won over Dan Cody during his teenage years, his success in the army during the First World War, and the connection he formed with Meyer Wolfshiem all testify to strengths of character. Nick Carraway became so intrigued by his neighbour that he has written a book telling his story, or at least Nick's own version of that story.

A01 Confident tone, and resourceful use of textual references to support point

A03 Thoughtful reference to literary context and conventions

Flawed he certainly is, but does Jay Gatsby really have the qualities of a tragic hero? In classical and Shakespearean tragedy heroes tend to be noble figures whose flawed character or poor judgement leads to their downfall. Gatsby has poor judgement: his obsession with Daisy is scarcely justified by anything we learn of her from Nick's characterisation. She appears shallow and cynical; her only ambition for her daughter Pammy is that she should become 'a beautiful little fool', which Daisy considers to be 'the best thing a girl can be in this world'. A Feminist critical reading might find more genuine tragedy in that feeble ambition than in the failure of Jay Gatsby's dream.

A05 Astute critical point, forcefully made

The fact that Gatsby does dream is part of his appeal for Nick, who himself fantasises about 'romantic women' he sees on the streets of New York, although his relationships with Jordan Baker and the girl he left behind in the Midwest both amount to nothing. Measured against 'the last and greatest of all human dreams', mentioned at the end of the novel, where Nick imagines a Dutch sailor discovering a New World, his own and Gatsby's fantasies seem painfully narrow and self-serving. What is it, after all, that Gatsby hopes to achieve? Nick suggests that Gatsby understood that once he had kissed Daisy 'and forever wed his unutterable visions to her perishable breath, his mind would never romp again like the mind of God'. Those 'unutterable visions' that drive Gatsby could never be satisfied by marriage to a flesh-and-blood woman.

A01 Very strong paragraph, weaving together useful textual details and quotes to make a persuasive and personally thought-through point

Nick notes at the start of the novel that Gatsby possessed 'an extraordinary gift for hope'. The problem is that he doesn't know what to hope for. Attaching that 'romantic readiness' to Daisy doesn't solve the problem. In her book 'Careless People' (2013), Sarah Churchwell quotes a statement by Zelda, wife of F. Scott Fitzgerald:

AO3 Very strong quote from secondary source and insightful point related to historical context

'We grew up founding our dreams on the infinite promise of American advertising.' That is a very revealing quotation as it suggests that the dreams of Americans living during the 1920s were manufactured; advertisements created desire for a better lifestyle and linked that improvement with objects that could be bought.

In that context Gatsby's desiring nature seems typical rather than extraordinary, a concentrated version of the desire felt by most Americans when confronted with the power of advertising. The significance of the eyes of Doctor Eckleburg, dominating the valley of ashes, becomes clear, and George Wilson's mistake in identifying that optician's hoarding with the eyes of God comes to seem like a form of truth. Advertising is the god of modern American mass society. Jay Gatsby, who is referred to as the son of God, 'about His Father's business', turns himself into a personification of advertising. His expensive clothes, imported cars and lavish parties are all examples of what the sociologist Thorstein Veblen called 'conspicuous consumption'. But they are also props that help to advertise the Gatsby brand, the new improved James Gatz.

AO1 Impressive point, using appropriate literary term

AO3 Very useful reference to historical context

A Marxist reading of 'The Great Gatsby' might argue that the transformation of America into a capitalist, consumer society was a collective tragedy. The New World, especially after the revolutionary break from Europe in 1776, might have offered an opportunity for unprecedented development of individual potential, in service of the collective good. Instead, the ideology of American individualism produced a mass consumer culture based on narrow self-interest, a society which despite its egalitarian ideals had in effect re-created the unjust class structure of the Old World, and we see this in the disparity between the lifestyles of the Buchanans and the Wilsons.

AO5 Astute reference to a critical perspective

AO3 Excellent contextual knowledge linked to the text

In his essay 'Tragedy and the Common Man' (1949), American playwright Arthur Miller argued that tragedy was not an old-fashioned genre that belonged to a former age of monarchs and aristocrats; ordinary people could be tragic heroes. The crucial quality, Miller argued, was that such heroes should be prepared to lay down their lives to preserve their 'sense of personal dignity'. I feel that Jay Gatsby's pursuit of Daisy lacks dignity, but his willingness to take the blame for the crime she commits in killing Myrtle is a dignified and redeeming act. As Nick says at the start of his narrative, 'Gatsby turned out all right at the end.'

AO4 Useful literary reference

AO1 Creative response weaving together literary context, personal critical angle and resourceful reference to the text

The student then goes on to discuss the question in relation to *Richard II*.

VERY HIGH LEVEL

Comment

- AO1 An impressively coherent and creatively personal response. In control of materials and of the construction of a persuasive argument.
- AO2 Use of quotations has a confidence that reflects an assured grasp of ways in which meaning is shaped in the text.
- AO3 Focused and refreshing engagement with historical context.
- AO4 Secondary literary and critical materials used with precision and purpose.
- AO5 Astute and assured reference to critical approaches and the light they might shed on central issues of the text.

PRACTICE TASK

Now it's your turn to work through an exam-style task on *The Great Gatsby*. The key is to:

- Quickly read and decode the task/question
- Briefly plan your points – then add a few more details, such as evidence, or make links between them
- Write your answer

Decode the question

> **'All tragedies are based on illusion.'** To what extent do you agree with this view in relation to *The Great Gatsby*, in terms of how it is constructed by its writer?

'All tragedies … illusion'	suggests that a common element in tragedy is 'illusion'
'illusion'	can mean 'trickery or magic' but here could also mean 'self-deception' (only seeing what one wants to see, rather than the truth)
'To what extent do you agree?'	What is my view? Do I agree with the statement completely, partially or not at all?
'constructed by its writer'	What has Fitzgerald done that supports (or doesn't support) this idea?

Plan and write

- Decide your viewpoint
- Plan your points
- Think of key evidence and quotations
- Write your answer

Success criteria

- Show your understanding of the idea of tragedy as a genre
- Draw on a range of critical views or different interpretation as appropriate
- Sustain your focus on the idea of 'illusion'
- Argue your **point of view** clearly and logically
- Make perceptive points and express your ideas confidently
- Support your points with relevant, well-chosen evidence including quotations
- Use literary terminology accurately and appropriately with reference to the effect on the reader
- Write in fluent, controlled and accurate English

Once you have finished, use the **Mark scheme** on page 112 to evaluate your response.

FURTHER READING

Biographies

Matthew J. Bruccoli, *Some Sort of Epic Grandeur: The Life of F. Scott Fitzgerald*, University of South Carolina Press, 2002

A highly readable and authoritatively informative biography, which conveys a vivid sense of F. Scott Fitzgerald and his time. Contains photographs

Arthur Mizener, *F. Scott Fitzgerald* (Literary Lives), Thames & Hudson, 1987

An approachable account of Fitzgerald's life and assessment of his achievement, illustrated with contemporary photographs

General reading

Andrew Blades, *York Notes Companions: Twentieth-Century American Literature*, York Press and Pearson, 2011

Jerome Charyn, *Gangsters and Gold Diggers: Old New York, the Jazz Age and the Birth of Broadway*, Four Walls Eight Windows, 2004

Captures the flavour of the place and the epoch with suitable zest

Maldwyn A. Jones, *American Immigration*, University of Chicago Press, 1992

Illustrated history of the process of immigration that created modern America

D. H. Lawrence, *Studies in Classic American Literature*, Penguin, 1977; first published 1923

Published before *The Great Gatsby* and concerned with nineteenth-century literature, but it offers very helpful insights into the nature of American idealism and American materialism

R. W. B. Lewis, *The American Adam: Innocence, Tragedy, and Tradition in the Nineteenth Century*, University of Chicago Press, 1955

This is a classic study of the recurrence of the biblical figure of Adam as a thematic touchstone in nineteenth-century American literature. Lewis shows that Gatsby, F. Scott Fitzgerald's deeply **ironic** Adam, had numerous precursors in American writing

Leo Marx, *The Machine in the Garden: Technology and the Pastoral Ideal in America*, Oxford University Press, 1964

An informative study of literary responses to technology in light of the widely held view of the American West as an unspoilt garden. Marx includes a brief discussion of *The Great Gatsby*

Lucy Moore, *Anything Goes: A Biography of the Roaring Twenties*, Atlantic, 2009

An atmospheric and illuminating account of the liberated and sometimes lawless lifestyle of the Jazz Age

Henry Nash Smith, *Virgin Land: The American West as Symbol and Myth*, Harvard University Press, 1971

Smith tells how the West acquired profound significance within America's perception of itself

Susan Strasser, *Satisfaction Guaranteed: The Making of the American Mass Market*, Pantheon, 1989

An entertaining and informative history of the emergence of consumerism in America, which contains much that is pertinent to *The Great Gatsby*

Critical studies

Ronald Berman, *The Great Gatsby and Modern Times*, University of Illinois Press, 1994

Places the novel in the context of its time and place

Harold Bloom, ed., *Gatsby*, Chelsea House, 1991

A series of provocative and stimulating essays

Sarah Churchwell, *Careless People: Murder, Mayhem and the Invention of* The Great Gatsby, Virago, 2013

From newspaper reports and other contemporary documents Churchwell weaves an entertaining and illuminating account of the context within which *The Great Gatsby* took shape

Jeffrey Louis Decker, 'Gatsby's Pristine Dream: The Diminishment of the Self-Made Man in the Tribal Twenties', *Novel*, Fall 1994, pp. 52–71

An essay which engages critically with issues of race raised by the novel

Morris Dickstein, ed., *Critical Insights: The Great Gatsby*, Salem Press, 2009

A collection that traces the critical reception of the novel from early reviews, troubled by its perceived immorality, to its current reputation as a literary masterpiece

Scott Donaldson, ed., *Critical Essays on F. Scott Fitzgerald's* The Great Gatsby, G. K. Hall, 1984

An invaluable collection of key documents in the history of criticism of *The Great Gatsby*

Hugh Kenner, *A Homemade World: The American Modernist Writers*, Johns Hopkins University Press, 1989

A discussion of F. Scott Fitzgerald and his contemporaries by a major literary critic

Katie de Koster, ed., *Readings on* The Great Gatsby, Greenhaven Press, 1997

A useful collection of essays from several decades, shedding light on the cultural context as well as literary form

A. Robert Lee, ed., *Scott Fitzgerald: The Promises of Life*, St Martin's Press, 1989

Varied selection of new essays on F. Scott Fitzgerald and his work

Robert E. Long, *The Achieving of* The Great Gatsby: *F. Scott Fitzgerald, 1920–25*, Bucknell University Press, 1979

Primarily a study of literary influences, especially that of Joseph Conrad

Lois Tyson, *Critical Theory Today: A User-friendly Guide*, second edition, Routledge, 2006

A very accessible introduction to critical approaches. Tyson offers helpful and illuminating Feminist, Marxist, Psychoanalytic and other readings of *The Great Gatsby*

Carlyle Van Thompson, 'Jay Gatsby's Passing in F. Scott Fitzgerald's *The Great Gatsby*', in *The Tragic Black Buck: Racial Masquerading in the American Literary Imagination*, Peter Lang, 2004, pp. 75–103

A provocative attempt by a distinguished African-American academic 'to make you think about a timeless and widely read novel as you never have before'

LITERARY TERMS

ambivalence the coexistence in one person of two different attitudes to the same object or wish

archetype (adj. **archetypal**) a character, action, situation or pattern that seems to represent a universal aspect or quality of human life

dialogue fictional conversation; words spoken between characters

foreshadow to give an anticipatory indication, or to hint at what will follow later in the narrative

irony the quality of an utterance or an event which appears to signify one thing but in fact conveys a meaning other than the obvious

metaphor describing one thing as being another. This goes further than a simile by merging two objects, for example 'the soldier was a lion in battle'

mythic belonging to myth, that is to stories that lay claim to truth beyond the influence of historical circumstances

narrative an account of events and action; or events and action that tell a story

narrator the voice within a written account or story that communicates the account or story to its readers; most simply, the teller of a tale

oxymoron a figure of speech which combines two apparently contradictory terms, for example 'a wise fool'

pastoral originally referring to the life led by shepherds, pastoral is the name given to a literary genre in which a simple way of life is compared favourably with a more complex way of life

point of view the way in which a narrator positions herself or himself in order to approach the materials forming a narrative and deliver them to readers. Examining the point of view helps us to understand how events are filtered through the narrator

realism set of conventions which enables representation of knowable communities and knowable characters

romance a narrative that departs from the dictates of reality as it is known to common sense in order to evoke a magical world (see the description taken from Nathaniel Hawthorne on p. 42)

simile a kind of metaphorical writing in which one thing is said to be like another thing. Similes always compare two things and contain the words 'like' or 'as'. For example: 'the soldier was like a lion in battle'

tragedy a play or other literary work depicting the downfall of its main character, due to an error of judgement, moral flaw or adverse circumstances

REVISION TASK ANSWERS

Task 1: Nick as character and as narrator

- Nick, who tells us that he was 'rather literary in college' (p. 10), has returned home to the Midwest and is writing a book about people he met a few years earlier in New York.
- In New York, Nick lived amongst the wealthy and glamorous, but although related to Daisy he is conscious that he does not really belong to that privileged class.
- Although Nick does not present himself as a romantic figure, Daisy teases him about a girl he left behind in the Midwest, and with her own plans to marry him to Jordan Baker.
- Gatsby fascinates Nick, who admires his 'extraordinary gift for hope' (p. 8), although he hints from the start that there is a sinister side to his neighbour.
- Nick tells us he is 'inclined to reserve all judgements' (p. 7), yet his descriptions of Tom and Daisy, which are generally unflattering, colour the way we see them.

Task 2: Gatsby's parties

- Gatsby's extravagant parties are part of the image he wishes to project, and are staged in the hope of impressing Daisy, who lives across the bay.
- 'People were not invited – they went there' (p. 43), Nick tells us, and Gatsby does not mix with his guests or drink and dance as they do.
- Despite the fact that Prohibition was in force during the 1920s, alcohol flows freely at Gatsby's parties.
- Gatsby's guests, who conduct themselves 'according to the rules of behaviour associated with an amusement park' (p. 43), embody the pleasure-seeking spirit of the Jazz Age.
- Nick and Gatsby share memories of the First World War, the horrors and deprivations of which form the grim historical backdrop to the self-indulgent excesses of the 1920s.

Task 3: Dishonesty and injustice

- The gangsters in this novel are based upon real figures in 1920s America, who broke the law and often acted violently in order to get rich.
- Wolfshiem is Jewish, which reflects the historical fact that gangsters tended to belong to ethnic communities who had restricted access to power, wealth and influence.
- Meyer Wolfshiem has fixed the outcome of the 1919 World Series, corrupting the spirit of honesty within sport.
- It is alleged that Gatsby is a bootlegger, so even the hero of this novel seems to have broken the law in order to get rich.
- Awareness of the disparity between the lifestyles of wealthy and poor Americans fuelled Gatsby's desire to leave his past behind.

Task 4: Gatsby in love

- Gatsby is anxious at the prospect of meeting Daisy again; he opens Nick's front door 'nervously' (p. 81).
- His tries to maintain his cool image through his immaculate clothing and care for the appearance of Nick's house, but 'there were dark signs of sleeplessness beneath his eyes' (p. 81).

- Nick tells Gatsby he is 'acting like a little boy' (p. 85), which emphasises the fact that, in terms of his emotions, Gatsby is trapped in his own past.
- Daisy experiences emotional turmoil, and although she attributes her tears to Gatsby's 'beautiful shirts' (p. 89) her response is rooted in memories and deep feelings.
- Watching Gatsby, Nick recognises 'the colossal vitality of his illusion' (p. 92), which goes far beyond the reality of Daisy, and has become self-sustaining.

Task 5: Role models

- James Gatz's imagination was too strong to allow him to settle into the lifestyle of his parents, who were 'shiftless and unsuccessful farm people' (p. 95).
- Farming is necessarily a settled way of life, with fixed routines, and that doesn't suit Gatsby's youthful restlessness.
- Dan Cody lives on a yacht, which has the attraction of physical mobility and represents for Gatsby 'all the beauty and glamour in the world' (p. 96).
- Cody's lifestyle as a prospector requires a 'gift for hope', which Nick has identified as a key characteristic of Gatsby (p. 8).
- Cody's heavy drinking reveals to Gatsby the addictive nature of alcohol, which he avoids himself but turns to his advantage as a bootlegger.

Task 6: Understanding the Buchanans

- Daisy enjoys showing off Pammy, as though she were some prize possession, and she speaks of her as an 'absolute little dream' (p. 112); her affection for the child seems artificial.
- Entrusted to a nurse, whose hand she holds, Pammy casts a 'reluctant backward glance' towards her mother (p. 112), suggesting she is not comfortable in her relationship with Daisy.
- Tom recognises Gatsby as a threat to his marriage and tries to belittle him, notably by referring to him as 'Mr Nobody from Nowhere' (p. 123).
- Tom's jealous response suggests possessiveness rather than love, ownership rather than affection.
- In light of his own adulterous behaviour Tom's defence of 'family life and family institutions' (p. 124) appears deeply **ironic**, especially as it leads to a racist remark.

Task 7: The human side of Gatsby

- Henry C. Gatz is presented as a modest figure, but his unassuming humanity has a reality that is lacking from his son's 'Platonic conception of himself' (p. 95).
- The pride Gatz takes in his son's achievement is poignant and ironic given the nature of that success and the fact that it followed Gatsby's rejection of his parents.
- But Gatz reveals that Gatsby returned to the Midwest two years previously and bought him the house he now lives in.
- The phrase 'I et like a hog' (p. 165) emphasises Gatz's lack of sophistication, especially when compared with Nick's educated and refined use of language.
- Yet Gatz and Nick are drawn together in their loyalty to Gatsby's memory, while other characters such as the Buchanans and Wolfshiem do not attend his funeral.

Task 8: Gatsby and America

- Gatsby's attempt to leave the past behind and invent a new identity based on a dream of a better future may be seen as parallel to America's break with Europe.
- But Gatsby's house and furnishings imitate European models, his clothes and cars are imported from the Old World, and social class remains a reality for characters in the novel.
- Gatsby's journey from a farm in the rural Midwest to the city of New York may be seen as a parallel to the historical development of America into a modern urban nation.
- The American Dream of success achieved through individual endeavour is seen in the novel to have been reduced to a desire to get rich quickly, and Gatsby's wealth is built upon crime.
- Along with the fashionable settings of West and East Egg, Fitzgerald's New York contains a valley of ashes, revealing a harsh reality beneath the surface glamour.

Task 9: Gatsby's desire

- The emotional behaviour of Gatsby and Daisy when they meet at Nick's house reveals the persistence of deep feelings between them.
- But when he first met her in Louisville Gatsby's perception of Daisy was coloured by his romantic imagination of 'radiant activities' taking place within her house (p. 141).
- In a moment of uncharacteristic **realism** Gatsby says of Daisy, 'Her voice is full of money', which prompts Nick to see her in a new light, as 'the king's daughter' (p. 115).
- Gatsby's devotion to Daisy finds a focal point in a green light, which like the 'fresh, green breast of the new world' (p. 171) is an image of unlimited potential rather than a well-defined goal.
- Gatsby's imagination exceeds Daisy's reality; once he had 'wed his unutterable visions to her perishable breath, his mind would never romp again like the mind of God' (p. 107).

Task 10: A man writing a book

- At the start of his **narrative** Nick makes it clear that, having returned to the Midwest, he is writing an account of events that occurred in New York a few years earlier.
- Nick remarks that he was 'rather literary in college' (p. 10), and his writing style draws attention to itself, notably in terms of sophisticated vocabulary and poetic images.
- In New York Nick was employed in the financial sector, a hard-headed and materialistic job that clearly did not satisfy the imaginative side of his nature.
- Everything we know about all the characters in this novel has been filtered through Nick's narration, which is the voice of a man with literary leanings.
- Arguably the key to Gatsby's attraction for Nick was that he appeared an ideal subject for a book, thus enabling Nick to reinvent himself as a writer.

Task 11: Style and substance

- An eco-critical approach might start with the image of 'a fresh, green breast of the new world' (p. 171), promising a fresh start in an unspoilt natural environment.
- The green light which becomes an object of fascination for Gatsby might be interpreted as a drastically diminished and artificial version of the 'fresh, green breast' (p. 171).
- The neat lawns of West and East Egg, and the gardeners who tidy the grounds of Gatsby's house in readiness for his parties, indicate how human taste imposes its order on Nature.
- The account of Gatsby's early years on the shores of Lake Superior, where his 'brown, hardening body lived naturally' (p. 95), shows him in harmony with his environment.
- The 'valley of ashes' (p. 26), where the Wilsons live and work, is a graphic image of the corruption of the natural world which supports the glamorous lifestyle of the wealthy.

PROGRESS CHECK ANSWERS

Part Two: Studying *The Great Gatsby*

Section One: Check your understanding

1.

- For: Nick is involved in the action and knew the other characters.
- For: He tells us he reserves judgement, which suggests he weighs up the evidence rather than rushing to a hasty conclusion.
- Against: But Jordan Baker expresses disappointment that Nick is not, as she had thought, 'an honest, straightforward person' (p. 168).
- Against: Nick does not tell us all he knows or feels, especially in relation to his own love affairs and romantic desires.

2.

- Nick is Daisy's second cousin once removed.
- He refers repeatedly to the quality of her voice, which he clearly finds highly attractive.

- But his account of her behaviour does not conceal her shallowness and lack of purpose.
- Daisy compares Nick to a rose (p. 19) – one of several statements that show her to be out of touch with reality.

3.

- Daisy shows Nick and Jordan her bruised knuckle, indicating her delicate physique and the strength of Tom who accidentally caused the bruising.
- Tom breaks Myrtle's nose, which shows his brutality.
- Wolfshiem recalls the shooting of a gangster named Rosenthal, which reflects actual violence on the streets of New York.
- Gatsby's car kills Myrtle, which shows how apparently beneficial technology can have harmful effects.
- George Wilson murders Gatsby, which shows that incorrect interpretations of events can have tragic consequences.

4.

- Gatsby's feelings for Daisy are trapped in the past and do not adequately take into account the passage of time during which she has married and had a child.
- Gatsby's 'Platonic conception of himself' (p. 95) belongs in an ideal world rather than to physical reality.

- But Tom's adulterous behaviour suggests that it might not be entirely unrealistic for Gatsby to hope that Daisy might leave her husband.
- After the death of Myrtle, Gatsby selflessly takes the blame, even though Daisy was driving the car, and that is a practical demonstration of his love for Daisy.

5.

- A key part of the American Dream is the freedom to leave the past behind and start a new life.
- The Frontier and the West have played a key role in this dream of new beginnings, but Dan Cody's story shows the Frontier spirit in a negative light.
- George Wilson hopes to move West with his wife and start a new life, but death is his only route out of the valley of ashes.
- Gatsby's new start was based on a sense of unlimited potential, but the scope of his life narrows down to a disastrous obsession with Daisy.
- Through his account of Gatsby's life and death Nick reinvents himself as a writer.

6.

- Gatsby's parties display the pleasure-seeking spirit of the Jazz Age.
- The liberated behaviour of young women attending these parties is a significant aspect of this period in American history.
- Heavy indulgence in alcohol is characteristic of Jazz Age behaviour, despite Prohibition being in force during the 1920s.
- A desire to live in the moment, evident in Jazz Age parties, also contributes to the novel's thematic concern with the passage of time.
- References to the First World War remind us of the grim and tragic historical events against which the indulgence of the Jazz Age was a reaction.

7.

- The American Civil War (1861–5) – avoided by Nick's great-uncle, who set up the family business, but a war which exposed serious flaws in the fabric of American society.
- The fixing of the 1919 World Series – sheds light on Gatsby's connections with the criminal underworld.
- The 'rush for metal' (p. 96) and especially the discovery of copper in Montana during the 1880s – the means by which Dan Cody got rich.
- Prohibition (1920–33), banning the production and sale of alcohol – which enabled Gatsby to get rich through the unlawful practice of bootlegging.

8.

- Gatsby claims to recognise Nick from their time in the army (p. 48) – shows his ability to win the confidence of another person, and perhaps also his skill at manipulating their response.
- Gatsby introduces Nick to Wolfshiem (Chapter 4) – reveals his criminal connections, while also emphasising Gatsby's personal charm.
- Nick accuses Gatsby of 'acting like a little boy' (p. 85) – Gatsby's cool image has fallen apart and the immaturity of the turbulent emotional life it has concealed becomes clear.
- Gatsby keeps a moonlit 'vigil' (p. 138) outside Tom and Daisy's house – displaying his love for Daisy, or perhaps fulfilling his own chivalric expectations of himself as a modern-day knight in the service of a lady.

9.

- There is no direct presentation of the death, which avoids melodrama and sensationalism, while also creating a sense of Gatsby's absence.
- The narration at this point is episodic: a brief account of

George Wilson arriving in West Egg is juxtaposed with a description of Gatsby floating in his pool.
- The murder is conveyed through the image of 'a thin red circle in the water' (p. 154).
- Gatsby's chauffeur hears the shots, but being a member of Wolfshiem's social circle he does not find the sound of gunfire a matter for particular concern.

10.

- Nick is a well-educated man, as may be seen from his taste for words such as 'contiguous' (p. 27), 'obsterical' (p. 52) and 'meretricious' (p. 95).
- As a young man Nick had literary leanings, and in his early thirties he still has a taste for poetic imagery, such as comparison of Gatsby's guests to 'moths among the whisperings and the champagne and the stars' (p. 41).
- Nick's descriptions of Gatsby's obsessive love for Daisy are crafted with such care that they often suggest that he feels comparable emotion himself, and may even share that attraction to Daisy.

11.

- Gatsby's parties reflect the pleasure-seeking spirit of the Jazz Age, and the extravagance of the wealthy.
- Description of these parties adds to our sense of Gatsby as a man set apart from the crowd, pursuing his own agenda and detached from the events surrounding him.
- Yet the nature of the parties shows Gatsby's skill as a kind of stage director, organising the music, lighting props and cast of a drama intended to impress Daisy, across the bay.
- The self-indulgence of many of the guests at these parties seems to provide a contrast to Gatsby's purposeful pursuit of Daisy, but on reflection that may be no less self-indulgent.

12.

- Daisy's name suggests a delicate flower, decorative rather than useful.
- Myrtle's name suggests a shrub, far sturdier and more resilient than a daisy, but it is also significant that in Greek mythology myrtle was a plant sacred to Aphrodite, the goddess of love.
- Dan Cody's surname is clearly intended to recall William Cody, known as Buffalo Bill, who turned the Wild West into a popular entertainment spectacle during the 1880s.
- Owl Eyes is a nickname suggesting defective vision, requiring rectification by means of glasses, but also wisdom, often associated with the owl, symbol of Athena, ancient Greek goddess of wisdom.

13.

- The entire narrative is an act of remembering, reconnecting Nick as **narrator**, living in the Midwest, to events that occurred in New York in 1922.
- At the party in Tom's apartment, Myrtle recalls the first time she met him on a train, and the attraction of his fashionable appearance – a parallel perhaps to Gatsby's first encounter with Daisy.
- Remembering his son's youth Henry C. Gatz remarks, 'Jimmy was bound to get ahead' (p. 164), yet the self-discipline of his 'schedule' was displaced by the lawless imaginings of Gatsby.
- Meyer Wolfshiem recalls the 'old Metropole' (p. 68) where Rosy Rosenthal was murdered – an oddly sentimental attachment which perhaps sheds light on Gatsby's own relationship with the past.

14.

- The hedonism of the Jazz Age can be interpreted as a reaction to the hardships and deprivations endured during the First World War.
- Nick served in the war, 'came back restless' (p. 9) and moved to

New York, feeling unable to settle in the Middle West.

- Gatsby 'did extraordinarily well in the war' (p. 143) and was promoted to major, which helped him subsequently to make useful, if disreputable, social connections.

- During Gatsby's absence in Europe, at the end of the war, Daisy married Tom Buchanan.

15.

- Henry C. Gatz attends his son's funeral, an embodiment of the humble Midwestern lifestyle Gatsby left behind.

- Owl Eyes turns up, expressing sympathy for a man he both admired and pitied, in a manner that might suggest a Fool in a Shakesperean tragedy.

- Nick remains a loyal friend, which suggests a level of identification with Gatsby's character that he does not openly admit, perhaps even to himself.

16.

- After giving birth to her daughter Pammy, Daisy said to a nurse that the best thing a girl can be in this world is 'a beautiful little fool' (p. 22).

- Daisy hears a bird in her garden and suggests it is 'a nightingale' (p. 20), showing her tendency to make romantic associations without foundation in reality.

- When Tom expresses racist views concerning a threat posed by non-white people, Daisy is complicit, whispering 'We've got to beat them down' (p. 18).

- Overcome with emotion during her reunion with Gatsby, Daisy tries to conceal the cause of her sobbing by commenting on the beauty of his shirts (p. 89).

17.

- In this novel New York is presented as modern, materialistic and constantly changing.

- In this novel the Midwest is presented as conventional, traditional and reserved.

- New York is associated with invidual desires and gratification.

- The Midwest is associated with family and communal values.

18.

- The motor car is a symbol of modernity and mobility.

- Gatsby's cars, one of which is a Rolls-Royce, are status symbols that testify to his wealth.

- Gatsby's car kills Myrtle Wilson, indicating that technological innovation can have tragic as well as beneficial consequences.

- The distinctive nature of Gatsby's vehicle makes it identifiable as the car that has caused Myrtle's death.

19.

- Young Jay Gatsby travels on board Dan Cody's yacht to the West Indies and the Barbary Coast, places that further fuelled his dissatisfaction with life in the Midwest.

- Nick and Gatsby travel to Europe to fight in the First World War, a life-changing event for both men.

- Nick identifies the Midwest with the 'thrilling returning trains' of his youth (p. 167), the sense of returning home.

20.

- Nick is narrator of the story and our knowledge of all the events and characters within it is filtered through him.

- Within his own narrative Nick tells us that he is not just telling the story but writing it, which indicates an element of literary self-awareness, a sense of style and technique.

- Nick Carraway is a character created by F. Scott Fitzgerald.

- Fitzgerald not only uses Nick to tell the story of Gatsby but also reflects, through this fictional character, on the nature of literary composition and the role of the author.

Section Two: Working towards the exam

1.

- Everything we know as readers is filtered through Nick, so we need to feel we can trust him as narrator to tell us the facts, rather than make things up.

- There are some references to places and to historical figures and events that can be verified as fact, although their presence in the novel is still reliant upon Nick's narrative voice.

- *The Great Gatsby* has aspects in common with detective fiction, with Nick sifting through the evidence and the gossip ('he killed a man once'; 'he was a German spy during the war', p. 45).

- Nick claims to be honest, but near the end of the book Jordan Baker disputes that, and if she finds him dishonest can we regard him as a reliable narrator?

- Other elements in the novel, especially those relating to Nick's love life, should lead us to suspect that he is not telling us everything, or is putting a personal slant on the facts.

- We should remain aware that *The Great Gatsby* is indeed a work of fiction, composed with literary skill by F. Scott Fitzgerald.

- But a crucial point, conveyed by Fitzgerald's technique, is that there is no absolute truth, that a **point of view** always enters into our grasp of facts and may be weaving them into fiction.

2.

- The entire novel is an act of memory, in that Nick is looking back at events that happened in New York a few years earlier.

- Memory, involving a sense of the past, provides a thematic contrast with the unreflecting quest for instant gratification shown by guests at Gatsby's Jazz Age parties.

- Memory also contrasts with gossip and rumour, which may be classed as false memories.

- But memory is not always presented in a positive light; Wolfshiem's recollection of the shooting of the gangster Rosenthal imposes a sentimental gloss on violent action.

- The First World War was an enormous upheaval for Nick, a rupture between the past when the Midwest seemed to be 'the warm centre of the world' and the post-war years when it seemed like 'the ragged edge of the universe' (p. 9).

- But shared memories of their time in the army form a bond between Nick and Gatsby and perhaps help to explain Nick's loyalty to his neighbour.

- Sharing memories may perhaps be the motivation for Nick to write, rather than his inward-looking desire to be a literary artist.

3.

- The 1920s and 1930s are often referred to as the 'Golden Age of Detective Fiction', with writers such as Raymond Chandler and Dashiell Hammett establishing the genre in America.

- Nick Carraway resembles a first-person narrator in detective fiction in the way he pieces evidence together and slowly reveals it to his readers.

- 'I'm inclined to reserve all judgements', Nick declares at the start of his account (p. 7), which establishes his credentials, in terms of character, to undertake detective work.

- Gatsby's connections within the criminal underworld place Nick's narrative in a context comparable to that found in a lot of detective fiction.

- Emphasis is placed on the air of mystery surrounding Gatsby, which provides fertile ground for detective work.

- Nick's account gradually dispels the mystery, yet still manages to sustain a kind of suspense as we read on to find out how the action unfolds.

4.

- A moral centre implies a commonly held set of values, or agreed terms for judging what is right and what is wrong.
- But the central character in this novel, described as 'great' in its title, is a man who seems to have got rich through criminal activity.
- Moreover, although the narrator is a man who prides himself on being honest, there are reasons to suspect that at times he is being, if not exactly dishonest, far from open and straightforward.
- Gatsby is unswervingly devoted to Daisy, yet she appears a superficial character and allows Gatsby to take the blame for Myrtle's death, although she was actually driving the car.
- George Wilson murders Gatsby, yet it is difficult not to feel sympathy for Wilson, whose wife committed adultery with Tom, a brutal man from a far more privileged social class.
- The supporting cast of characters, notably Wolfshiem and Dan Cody, but also the numerous guests at Gatsby's parties, display little, if any, moral awareness.
- Fitzgerald's novel conveys a sense that Americans in the years after the First World War were a Lost Generation, as Gertrude Stein put it, drifting aimlessly and without moral direction.

5.

- The story of Gatsby is framed by Nick's own narrative (briefly told in the book), in which he has returned home to the Midwest in order to write an account of events that took place a few years earlier.
- The dynamics of Gatsby's story are determined by his 'extraordinary gift for hope' (p. 8), looking towards the future, and his dedication to Daisy, as he remembers her in the past.
- Although Nick's narrative moves towards a culminating point – the death of Gatsby and its aftermath – it is not told in a continuous and linear way, but is episodic, revealing details from the more distant past.
- Use of the scenic method and **dialogue** creates a sense that we are watching events as they occur in the present.
- 'So we beat on, boats against the current, borne back ceaselessly into the past' (p. 172) – Nick's concluding statement distils into a single sentence the complex relationship of past, present and future that has been evident throughout the preceding account.

Part Three: Characters and themes

Section One: Check your understanding

1.

- Gatsby is a close friend of the gangster Meyer Wolfshiem.
- Gatsby receives phone calls from shadowy figures in Chicago.
- Rumour about his bootlegging activities is fuelled by his considerable wealth, acquired mysteriously and quickly.

2.

- Against: Gatsby has charm and glamour.
- Against: Nick takes pride in being honest and straightforward.
- For: Gatsby has friends in the criminal underworld and is rumoured to be a bootlegger.
- For: Jordan Baker tells Nick that he is not honest and straightforward.

3.

- Pammy is a physical embodiment of the time that has passed since Daisy married Tom rather than Gatsby.

- Pammy is 'well-disciplined' (p. 112), unlike most of the adults in this novel.
- Daisy calls Pammy an 'absolute little dream' (p. 112), but shows no real affection towards her, which adds to our sense of Daisy's superficiality.

4.

- The Buchanans live in fashionable and exclusive East Egg; the Wilsons live in the valley of ashes.
- The Buchanans have inherited wealth and lead leisurely lives; the Wilsons have to work for a living.
- The Buchanans are able to travel wherever they want; the Wilsons are trapped in one place.
- The Buchanans have a child; the Wilsons are childless.

5.

- Daisy teases Nick about a young woman he has left behind in the Midwest – Nick acknowledges this relationship but is clearly unwilling to tell us what happened.
- Jordan says to Nick, 'You threw me over on the telephone' (p. 168) – the relationship between them had clearly developed, romantically, in ways that Nick doesn't disclose.
- Nick refers on several occasions to Daisy's 'low, thrilling voice' (p. 14) – he clearly recognises her seductive appeal; is Nick perhaps in love with Daisy?

6.

- America has recently been involved in the First World War, which indicates that a clean break with the European past has not occurred.
- The 'valley of ashes' (p. 26) blights the landscape, a product of industrialised and urban America and a betrayal of hopes that society would harmonise with Nature.
- The homes of the wealthy mimic the design and decor of houses built by the European aristocracy, which suggests the persistence of a class structure America hoped to leave behind.
- Tom's racist outburst, in which he identifies himself as a member of 'the dominant race' (p. 18), indicates a serious failure of America's egalitarian ideals.

7.

- Owl Eyes wears spectacles and drinks heavily, but although his physical vision might not be perfect he is a character who sees things clearly.
- The fact that Nick does not know the real name of Owl Eyes reminds us that Gatsby's parties are not gatherings of friends, but staged events involving lots of minor roles and supporting players.
- Owl Eyes admires Gatsby as a master of illusion – 'What throughness! What realism!' (p. 47).
- At Gatsby's funeral Owl Eyes casts doubt on the dead man's greatness: 'The poor son-of-a-bitch' (p. 166).

8.

- Gatsby stares across the bay at the green light which has become a focal point for his longing for Daisy.
- In Gatsby's house, Daisy starts to sob as she inspects his wardrobes of clothes; she pretends she is overcome by the beauty of his shirts (p. 89), but the real reason is her desire for him.
- Nick reveals that he liked to 'pick out romantic women from the crowd' on Fifth Avenue (p. 57) and imagine himself becoming involved with them.

9.

- American football, the sport in which Tom became a celebrity at college, temporarily imposed a set of rules on the way he used his 'cruel body' (p. 12).
- Tom owns 'a string of polo ponies' (p. 11), which not only allows

him to play this sport but also shows that he is living according to an upper-class code of conduct.

- Jordan has been accused of cheating in a golf tournament, although later she expresses disappointment at finding out that Nick is not 'an honest, straightforward person' (p. 168).
- Meyer Wolfshiem fixed the 1919 baseball World Series, which is not only a criminal act but a betrayal of the trust of followers of this mass spectator sport.

10.
- A tradition in Nick Carraway's family claims descent from the Dukes of Buccleuch (p. 8), which shows lingering attachment in America to Old World class distinctions.
- The name Buchanan suggests descent from an ancient Scottish clan and a long connection to the European past.
- Gatsby and the Buchanans employ servants, so even domestic work is done on their behalf.
- But the Wilsons struggle to make a living in the bleak surroundings of the valley of ashes.
- Jordan recalls meeting Tom and Daisy in the chic French resorts of Cannes and Deauville, which shows a freedom to travel unknown to working-class Americans such as the Wilsons or the Gatz family.

Section Two: Working towards the exam

1.
- Gatsby can be regarded as an embodiment of America in that he seeks to leave his past behind and create a new identity; comparably, America broke away from European rule.
- Gatsby looks to Europe for status symbols such as his Rolls-Royce and his clothes; comparably America, as presented in this novel, has a class structure that resembles that of the Old World it sought to leave behind.
- Gatsby pursues an ideal vision, but in order to achieve it he uses materialistic means, apparently involving criminal activity.
- America's ideals are also depicted by Fitzgerald as compromised by materialism.
- Gatsby rose in status after serving in the First World War.
- One of America's founding ideals was to remain a peaceful nation but participation in the First World War helped it to develop as an industrial nation and a power on the world stage.
- Gatsby is dead at the end of the novel, and Nick's concluding reference to Dutch sailors encountering the New World leaves a sense that America's ideals have met a similarly tragic fate.

2.
- The view of the 1920s we find in Fitzgerald's novel is inseparable from Nick's narration, and the implied judgements passed on modern America reflect Nick's character.
- Nick admires Gatsby's 'extraordinary gift for hope' (p. 8) and shows himself to be a pessimist with little to look forward to.
- It may be argued that his depiction of America as a land of failed dreams and broken relationships is a reflection of problems within his own life.
- The positive aspects of American culture – its energy, ingenuity and creativity – are less evident in Nick's **narrative** than its inequalities, corruption and violence.
- Jordan Baker's observation that Nick is a 'bad driver' (p. 168) suggests that his judgement should not be trusted without reservation.
- In light of this argument, we might conclude that Nick is attracted to Gatsby not because he is 'great' but because his life

is a tragic failure and Nick's pessimism – perhaps a consequence of his war service – leads him to find such failure attractive.
- Such a state of mind would inevitably colour Nick's view of modern American life.

3.
- Success might be defined in terms of the growth of the main character in the story, or of the **narrator** of the story.
- Mark Twain's Huckleberry Finn grows in sympathy for other human beings and develops in moral understanding.
- Huck Finn is unable to settle within the confines of society and 'lights out for the Territory', which may be interpreted as a failure to develop in the right way.
- Fitzgerald's Jay Gatsby resembles Twain's Tom Sawyer in his flawed grasp of reality and fantasising distortion of the present.
- Nick Carraway admires Gatsby's optimism, but he himself ends up disillusioned and pessimistic.
- Nick settles back into Midwestern life, which may be viewed as success if you value rootedness, but suggests failure if you believe that life is about continuing to develop rather than dwelling in the past.

Part Four: Genre, structure and language

Section One: Check your understanding

1.
- First-person narrator
- Framing **narrative**
- **Dialogue** – used to advance plot and characterisation
- Scenic method

2.
- Green – associated with Nature and the promise of the New World, but also the green light that Gatsby stares towards, which carries connotations of jealousy or envy.
- Breast – an image used **metaphorically** at the end of the novel in relation to wonder felt at the discovery of America, but also a literal reference to mutilation following Myrtle's death.
- Dust – literal dust surrounds the Wilsons in their everyday lives, but Nick also uses the word figuratively, referring to 'foul dust' (p. 8) that floated in the wake of Gatsby's dreams.

3.
- Fitzgerald's patterned use of colour and attention to changes of light at various times of day are aspects of the novel that lend themselves to cinematic representation.
- The scenic method, using sequences of action and dialogue set in specific locations almost as if in a play, might easily be adapted for a film version.
- But the subtle way in which Fitzgerald uses Nick as a (possibly unreliable) narrator, filtering all the information we receive through his own personality, would be difficult to re-create on screen.
- Nick's literary use of language, carefully patterned and sometimes poetic in its concentration, would be difficult to transfer to film.

4.
- Tragedy involves the downfall of a character initially perceived to be 'great'.
- This downfall is often caused by a character flaw or an error of judgement (in this case Gatsby's devotion to Daisy).

- As the narrative develops, events take on an air of tragic inevitability, appearing to carry Gatsby towards his inescapable downfall.
- Serious lessons, concerning the nature of society and life in the wider world, can be learnt from the personal tragedy of Jay Gatsby.

5.

- Daisy's family home in Louisville has, for Gatsby, an air of mystery and a suggestion of 'radiant activities' (p. 141), and his subsequent perceptions are coloured by imagination.
- Nick's literary self-consciousness results in prose that does not aim to capture details with photographic **realism**, but generates less tangible kinds of meaning.
- Nick makes explicit references to perceptions that belong to **romance** rather than realism; for example, 'A new world, material without being real, where poor ghosts, breathing dreams like air, drifted fortuitously about' (pp. 153–4).
- The narrative shows careful concern for qualities of light, and while harsh daylight might lend itself to realistic description the nature of reality in moonlit sequences is far less clear-cut.

6.

- The schedule drawn up by James Gatz in 1906 is intended to give order to each hour of the day, so as to ensure steady self-development and future success.
- Photographs (those McKee takes, the one of his son that Henry Gatz carries or the one of Myrtle's mother) involve the freezing of a moment of time within an image.
- 'Vladimir Tostoff's Jazz History of the World' (p. 51) is an **ironic** reference, as the pleasure-seeking spirit of the Jazz Age is directed to the present moment rather than the past.

7.

- Greatness is a conventional attribute of a tragic hero, so the title might lead us to expect the novel to be a tragedy.
- 'The Great Gatsby' is a phrase that suggests a showman, in the manner of the famous American illusionist Harry Houdini, who was known professionally as The Great Houdini.
- The First World War was widely known as The Great War, and given the numerous references to that conflict in the novel we associate 'Great' with collective as well as personal tragedy.
- In the novel itself, Henry Gatz says that his son tried to improve his mind, 'He was always great for that' (p. 165) – a more modest and colloquial use of the word.

8.

- Dialogue gives us the sense that we are listening directly to the voices of characters speaking, rather than having their meaning reported to us.
- Dialogue is one of the means by which a writer can develop characterisation, using accent, different kinds of language use or speech mannerisms to help us understand a character.
- Dialogue is one way of introducing memory into the text, as when Myrtle speaks about the first time she met Tom Buchanan, or when Gatsby and Nick reminisce about the recent war.

9.

- Teutonic – Germanic, relating to Germany
- Infinitesimal – extremely small
- Contingency – uncertainty; chance occurrence
- Meretricious – showy, superficially attractive but of no real value
- Platonic – relating to the Greek philosopher Plato; spiritual; aspiring to an ideal

10.

- The name of West Egg carries symbolic resonance of a new beginning, in terms of both the Frontier tradition of the American West and the life-bearing nature of an egg.
- George Wilson's mistaken identification of Doctor Eckleburg's hoarding with the eyes of God might suggest symbolically that advertising is all-powerful in 1920s America.
- The broken clock which Gatsby dislodges from Nick's mantlepiece (p. 84) may be seen as a symbol of Gatsby's dysfunctional relationship with the passage of time.

Section Two: Working towards the exam

1.

- Nick 'was rather literary in college' (p. 10), and the style and vocabulary of his account foreground that literariness.
- His father runs a solid, Midwestern hardware business and Nick has worked in finance, yet he was attracted to Gatsby, not least perhaps because his life provided material for the writing of a book.
- Gatsby's life may appear to have been wasted in pursuit of an unfulfilled dream, but by turning that life into a work of literature Nick has granted it far broader significance.
- Nick presents himself as melancholy and pessimistic, a man with nothing to look forward to but 'the promise of a decade of loneliness' (p. 129).
- But writing a book about Gatsby gives his own life purpose and value.
- The closing sentence of the book refers to the inexorable passage of time.
- But a work of literary art endures beyond the author's life and, in a sense, transcends time.

2.

- Playwright Arthur Miller suggested in 1949 that, in a modern democratic society, tragedy does not involve the fall of some great figure but the struggle of ordinary people to preserve their dignity.
- The title *The Great Gatsby* sets up this novel's hero as an exceptional man, but the terms of Gatsby's greatness are never clearly established and that title comes to appear ironic.
- If dignity is defined in terms of the right of individuals to develop their potential as fully as possible, then the schedule that Gatsby drew up as a boy might be regarded as a means to achieve dignity.
- But Gatsby follows another route to material success, apparently involving crime and deception.
- Gatsby's obsession with Daisy, after her marriage, may seem like chivalrous devotion, but when he meets her Nick notices Gatsby's undignified behaviour and says, 'You're acting like a little boy' (p. 85).
- Protecting Daisy by shouldering blame following the accident that kills Myrtle may seem like a dignified act, but the consequence is that Gatsby dies, and Daisy does not even attend his funeral.
- Perhaps by granting this series of events an air of tragedy in his narrative Nick is dignifying Gatsby's story, but a case might equally be made to suggest that interest in Gatsby calls Nick's own dignity into question.

3.

- Nick Carraway, from whose **point of view** this story is told, says that 'life is much more successfully looked at from a single window, after all' (p. 10).

- But in the telling Nick exposes the fact that Gatsby's story can be interpreted from a variety of points of view, some of which are conflicting.
- As a work of modernist literature, *The Great Gatsby* accepts that there is no absolute truth; other versions, alternative interpretations, different perspectives are always possible.
- William Faulkner's novel *The Sound and the Fury*, another modernist novel, embodies this plurality of readings through a series of three first-person narratives and a fourth that appears to offer a detached third-person overview.
- But Faulkner shows that point of view cannot be separated from the preferences and interests of the **narrator** – in the case of Benjy Compson, obsession with fire, the golf course and his sister Caddy.
- Faulkner shows that varying points of view involve not only different opinions, but different perceptions – Benjy sees and understands things in a different way from his Harvard-educated brother Quentin, for example.
- Reading *The Great Gatsby*, we need to take into account not only what Nick tells us but also the aspects of his character that shape and place limits upon his own point of view.

Part Five: Contexts and interpretations

Section One: Check your understanding

1.
- Cars – increase mobility and speed of travel, but also feature as machines that can kill.
- Telephones – allow instant communication across large distances, but are used in the novel to make adultery easier and possibly to arrange criminal activities.
- Electric lighting – enables Gatsby to enhance the glamour of his garden parties, but his fixation on the light across the bay is a key factor in his tragedy.

2.
- America is a post-colonial society, which declared independence from European states in 1776.
- Fitzgerald portrays America as a nation that still follows Old World models when looking for ways to define social status and success, e.g. in the design and decor of houses.
- Tom's racism, especially his reference to a book entitled *The Rise of the Coloured Empires*, shows the persistence in post-colonial America of belief in 'the dominant race' (p. 18).
- If Gatsby is interpreted as an embodiment of America, a post-colonial reading might see his tragedy to be that he suffers from the tyranny of the past.

3.
- Daisy speaks of a nightingale in the garden and compares Nick to a rose, suggesting that her sense of reality is distorted by romantic fantasies.
- Tom breaks Myrtle's nose, making explicit the abusive nature of his relationship with her.
- The phrase 'son-of-a-bitch', used on page 133 and again on page 166, is contemptuous of women, implying that objectionable characteristics of a man can be traced back to his mother.
- Daisy tells how she declared, just after Pammy's birth, that the best thing a girl can be is 'a beautiful little fool' (p. 22).
- A feminist reading might argue that Gatsby's act of staring across the bay, at Daisy's house, in effect turns her into the passive object of his gaze.

4.
- Nick's experience during the Great War leaves him feeling that his home in the Middle West is no longer 'the warm centre of the world' but now seems 'like the ragged edge of the universe' (p. 9).
- 'What do people plan?' (p. 17) asks Daisy, whose conversation often shows that her life lacks any clear purpose or direction.
- The large amount of alcohol consumed in this novel, at Gatsby's parties, but on other social occasions too, appears to be in part a response to boredom and a sense that life is meaningless.

5.
- Literary modernism flourished in the decades immediately before and after the First World War.
- Modernist novels published in the same year as *The Great Gatsby* include *Manhattan Transfer* by John Dos Passos and Virginia Woolf's *Mrs Dalloway*.
- Modernism is characterised in part by its self-conscious approach to form, technique and language, so modernist novels are concerned as much with the way a story is told as with the story itself.
- In modernist narratives truth is not absolute, fixed and self-evident, but is closely linked, as in Nick Carraway's narration, to point of view.
- Modernist narratives, which rarely unfold in a straightforwardly linear way, often exhibit a formal as well as a thematic concern with time.

6.
- Rather than looking at *The Great Gatsby* in isolation or only in relation to other literary works, a New Historicist approach draws on non-literary documents to shed light on the 1920s, or on the present in which the text is being read.
- For example, such a reading might examine Henry Ford's *My Life and Work*, published in 1922, the year in which the action of *The Great Gatsby* takes place.
- Ford's autobiography offers insights not only into the development of American industry and automobile production, but also into the standardisation of goods and regimentation of the workplace.
- Such information might be used in combination with Fitzgerald's depiction of mass society, and his novels focus upon a supposedly exceptional individual.
- Charlie Chaplin's film *Modern Times* (1936), a comedy which depicts an ordinary man working on a factory assembly line, might also be used as a contrast to Gatsby's romantic self-absorption.

7.
- Willa Cather's *My Ántonia* (1918) is set in the American Midwest; Nick Carraway and Jay Gatsby grew up in the same region.
- At the start of *The Great Gatsby* Nick Carraway tells us that he is writing this account; at the start of *My Ántonia* we are told that Jim Burden has written the account that follows.
- Gatsby grows up on his parents' farm, but leaves for the city (New York); Ántonia grows up on her parents' farm and stays, but another key character, Lena, leaves for the city (San Francisco).
- In *The Great Gatsby* cars are an indication of changing social relationships; in the final section of Cather's novel Ántonia remarks that her daughter has a Ford car, so 'she don't seem so far away from me as she used to.'

8.

- Sport has become a mass spectacle – Wolfshiem's fixing of the World Series affects many Americans.
- Newspapers and magazines have mass circulation – Henry Gatz reads of his son's death in a Chicago newspaper.
- Cars are being mass-produced – Gatsby buys a Rolls-Royce to stand out from the crowd.
- Robert Keable's novel *Simon Called Peter*, mentioned on page 31, is a best-seller – literature too is becoming a commodity in the market-place.
- The First World War – the organisation of troop movements reflected the mass nature of modern society, and American industry expanded due to the war's production demands.

9.

- The Civil War – the collapse of America's hopes of being a peaceful and harmonious society.
- The fixing of the baseball World Series in 1919 – a scandalous violation of sport's codes of conduct.
- The murder of Rosy Rosenthal at the Metropole – violent criminality within the context of everyday urban life.

10.

- James Gatz was born in America's Middle West; Jay Gatsby dies in New York.
- The Midwest economy was based in the routines of farm life; New York's economy is characterised by consumerism, advertising, mass production and financial transactions.
- James Gatz grew up in a world without telephones or cars; Gatsby makes use of both cars and telephones, which make distances seem to shrink.
- In his boyhood, clothes were practical and casual ('a torn green jersey and a pair of canvas pants', pp. 94–5); in his adult life clothing is a matter of image and fashion ('such beautiful shirts', p. 89).

Section Two: Working towards the exam

1.

- An eco-critical reading might argue that the Wilsons are dehumanised by processes of industrialisation and urbanisation that desecrate the natural environment.
- Such a reading might point out that by running a garage the Wilsons are actually serving the interests of the exploitative system that is steadily destroying them.
- A Feminist reading might focus upon the fact that Myrtle is economically dependent upon George.
- Her relationship with Tom Buchanan might then be interpreted as transferral of that dependency to a more powerful representative of the patriarchy.
- A Marxist interpretation might present the Wilsons as representatives of the working class, unable within the capitalist system to determine the conduct of their own lives.
- George's labour is in the service of members of a wealthier and more powerful class, and Myrtle's physical relationship with Tom, stripped of any pretence that Tom genuinely cares for her, might be seen in the same light.

2.

- The eyes of Doctor Eckleburg are an advertising hoarding and we see through them in the sense that this novel is pervaded by the power of advertising, including Gatsby's own self-advertisement.
- Advertising in modern consumer societies involves the creation of desire, and Gatsby promotes his own image in the hope of persuading Daisy that she needs him.
- Eckleburg's eyes see nothing, which reflects **ironically** on Gatsby's gaze, directed towards Daisy but actually looking beyond her towards some undefined and unreal goal.
- George Wilson mistakes the eyes of Eckleburg for the eyes of God, but *The Great Gatsby* depicts a world in which, as in Fitzgerald's earlier novel *This Side of Paradise*, we find 'all Gods dead'.
- We might argue, however, that advertising is the god of 1920s America, as depicted in this novel, where image and style have become all-important.
- Eckleburg's eyes are a fitting symbol for the decade when the visual entertainments of cinema and spectator sports were becoming established as favourite leisure activities of mass society.

3.

- Theodore Dreiser, in his **realist** novel *Sister Carrie* (1900), shows the cross-country railroad system to be, for Carrie Meeber, a means of escape from the rural Midwest.
- In *The Great Gatsby* Nick Carraway associates the Midwest with 'the thrilling returning trains of my youth' (p. 167).
- Dreiser depicts Carrie Meeber working as a machine operator in a Chicago shoe factory, a regimented workplace which turns human beings into cogs in a mechanical system.
- The leisured class depicted in *The Great Gatsby* have no contact with this mechanical system, yet they depend upon it for the continuance of their social privileges.
- George Hurstwood, in *Sister Carrie*, drives a streetcar in Brooklyn during a strike and provokes the anger of strikers – a vivid illustration of the social contexts and conflicts within which technology, in itself neutral, is used.
- George Wilson working at his garage is comparably caught up in a social context where technology has meanings and implications beyond its mere use; Gatsby's Rolls-Royce is a symbol of his affluence, for example.
- Electric lighting features significantly in *The Great Gatsby* and in *Sister Carrie*, where the illumination of the theatre and department store connotes the energy and excitement of modern city life.

MARK SCHEME

Use this page to assess your answer to the **Practice task** provided on page 100.

Look at the elements listed for each Assessment Objective. Examiners will be looking to award the highest grades to the students who meet the majority of these criteria. If you can meet two to three elements from each AO, you are working at a good level, with some room for improvement to a higher level.*

'All tragedies are based on illusion.' To what extent do you agree with this view in relation to *The Great Gatsby*, in terms of how it is constructed by its writer?

AO1	Articulate informed, personal and creative responses to literary texts, using associated concepts and terminology, and coherent, accurate written expression.	• You make a range of clear, relevant points about the illusions of a range of characters within the novel, for example Gatsby, Nick and the Wilsons. • You use a range of literary terms correctly, e.g. **foreshadowing**, **metaphor**, **romance**, **oxymoron**, **dialogue**. • You write a clear introduction, outlining your thesis and provide a clear conclusion. • You signpost and link your ideas fluently about tragedy and illusion within the novel. • You offer a personal interpretation which is well-argued and convincing.
AO2	Analyse ways in which meanings are shaped in literary texts.	• You explain the techniques and methods Fitzgerald uses to present illusion through description of setting (i.e the valley of ashes) and character (Gatsby's perspective on Daisy). • You explain in detail how such examples shape meaning, e.g. Nick's emphasis on Gatsby's 'extraordinary gift for hope' as a positive value but how this masks his misunderstanding of reality. • You comment on how the words spoken by individuals – George Wilson's plans to relocate; Gatsby's efforts to make his house impressive; or other dialogue – represent hopeless effort against the tragic impulse.
AO3	Demonstrate understanding of the significance and influence of the contexts in which literary texts are written and received.	• You demonstrate your understanding of tragic tropes and motifs – the 'hero' with a weakness that brings him down; the idea of hubris; the way events combine inexorably to bring about tragedy. • Literary context: Gatsby takes on a role from chivalric legend, but his fate reflects an irresolvable clash between romance and realism. • Historical context: Gatsby's route to wealth is connected to Prohibition, and to the violent and lawless underworld of American cities in the 1920s, the sense that the superficial glamour of Gatsby's life is an illusion which hides a dark underbelly.
AO4	Explore connections across literary texts.	• You make relevant links between characters and ideas, noting how for example Wilson's illusions mirror Gatsby's, albeit for different reasons presented in the novel.
AO5	Explore literary texts informed by different interpretations.	• Where appropriate, you incorporate and comment on critics' views of the extent to which the novel can be seen in tragic terms. • You assert your own independent view clearly.

* This mark scheme gives you a broad indication of attainment, but check the specific mark scheme for your paper/task to ensure you know what to focus on.